Picture Book for Zone • Cooks

Carolyn Brooks & Darlene Kvist

30% Protein | *40% Carbohydrates* | *30% Fats*

ACKNOWLEDGEMENTS

We want to give special thanks to everyone who contributed to this book, especially our clients and our In-Balance cooking class participants who tested these recipes, prepared them many times and offered valuable feedback concerning taste, preparation and cooking instructions. We gratefully acknowledge the assistance and inspiration provided by the following people:

Nancy Green– We appreciate your enthusiasm as a client; your adventurous spirit and eagerness to try every new idea we threw your way; your willingness to come out of retirement from teaching home economics to teach this balanced way of cooking with commitment and humor. Sampling your creations at our In-Balance cooking classes was always a special treat. Your constant devotion to this project and your recipe contributions were invaluable.

Anna Esser– We thank you for your enthusiastic participation at our classes; your encouragement to continue with this project –photos and all– your talent as a food stylist and your skills as a photographer that resulted in the wonderful photos adorning each recipe in this book.

Linda Newell– We admire your let's-get-this-done attitude; your belief in our program; your fantastic computer skills and dedication to long hours on the computer. Your ability to analyze nutrients, to fine-tune our cooking instructions and to "edit as you go" made the first edition of this cookbook a reality.

Jim Loughrey– Your commitment to this way of eating and continued encouragement as a client and class participant gave us the motivation to complete this project. Without your computer wizardry, printing capabilities and hours spent compiling the first edition, it would never have been completed. Your energy was the springboard we needed to get this second, revised edition off the ground.

Alana Ray– Who spent hours retyping the entire manuscript for the second printing so we could utilize the capabilities of our graphic artist.

Jan Joseph– Whose graphic arts wizardry redesigned this new edition and breathed life into the project.

And a special thanks to: Genevieve Goodwin and Evelyn Brooks, our Mothers, who fed us this way as children. We grew up eating balanced Zone-like meals. We bet most of our readers did, too. Thank you both for being so patient and sacrificing Mother-Daughter time with us so we could get this cookbook done on schedule.

1st Edition
Published by: Nutritional Weight & Wellness

Picture Book for Zone Cooks

CONTENTS

DEDICATION

*We dedicate this innovative **Picture Book for Zone Cooks** to all those cooks dedicated to making Zone meals and snacks a part of their everyday lifestyle and to all those we've worked with over the past 20 years who have continued to ask, "When are you going to put together a cookbook?"*

We have learned a great deal from all our clients: those we counsel individually; those who have attended our classes; and those who have come through our doors seeking to make lasting changes in the way they eat and how they relate to food. They come motivated by a desire to look and feel better, to increase their energy so they can enjoy life each day and to achieve a greater sense of emotional well-being.

We pride ourselves in educating our clients. It is important to us that they receive the information they need to empower them to make lasting lifestyle changes. Counseling clients over the past 20 years has taught us that the most effective way to help clients make long term changes in their eating habits is to help them understand how food effects their body, their mind and their emotions.

The easiest way to help people make a healthy eating plan part of their lifestyle is to make certain that they feel comfortable with the meals they are preparing for themselves and their families. The meals must taste good, must be easy to prepare and appealing to the eye.

First of all, the meals must taste good. The delicious recipes and meal plans to follow use common, easy to find ingredients that taste great. We have included a few convenient foods that taste great, but may be new to some readers. We like them because of their fantastic health benefits, lack of preservatives, ease of preparation and

healing properties. We urge you to try some of these new taste treats– ethnic whole grains like amaranth, quinoa and teff that are popular and easy to find today, and soy foods like tofu, tempeh and the textured vegetable protein products that have become popular meat replacements– by including them in one new recipe a week.

Healthy, healing meals must be easy to prepare if they are to become a part of your everyday lifestyle. Recipes in this Picture Book for Zone Cooks have passed the test of time. They represent the very best of those we've gathered over the past twenty years for both taste and ease of preparation. They have been tasted and tested and balanced to meet Zone guidelines by ourselves, our clients, and our cooking teacher, Nancy Green. Nancy has continued fine tuning the ingredients and the instructions, making them even easier to follow, each time she prepared meals for our cooking classes. They have been improved even more from feedback we received from the hundreds of students attending these classes during the past two years.

*Third, a new recipe must look good or you won't even try it! Because eye appeal is such an important part of enjoying a meal, you can be sure the recipes that follow are attractive– so attractive, in fact, we've included a picture of each one. Thus, this **Picture Book for Zone Cooks** grew from our desire to help everyone– not just those able to attend our classes– visualize what healing Zone meals look like. We hope all who discover this healing way of eating will continue to thrive on its benefits and learn to love it as much as we do.*

Thus, we dedicate this book to Zone cooks everywhere so they may picture healthy Zone meals with ease.

INTRODUCTION

Picture Book for Zone Cooks is a basic primer to teach you the fundamentals of planning your meals based on the concepts put forth in Dr. Barry Sear's popular books *The Zone* and *Mastering The Zone*. It provides you with the basics you need to become "literate" in Zone meal planning. It will teach you the building blocks of good nutrition based on the Zone blocks developed by Dr. Sears. It includes all the basics you will need to get started– a list of the most healing Zone foods– a shopping list for stocking your kitchen– easy to follow recipes--and guides to make planning your meals and snacks around the Zone food blocks as simple as child's play.

To function at your peak, mentally, physically and emotionally, your body needs the right fuels. When you fuel your body with balanced, healthy meals, you will look and feel better, become more balanced emotionally, and live a longer, more productive life.

We believe that food– the most powerful of medicines– must taste great, be easy to prepare and fun to eat, and if that food is balanced according to the formula set forth in *The Zone*, it is powerful medicine indeed. Therein lies our expertise– applying the principles and biochemistry behind Dr. Sear's book, *The Zone*, to attractive meals that can be prepared easily, use health promoting foods, taste delicious and promote healing.

In this age of drug technology with its emphasis on better living through chemicals, the powerful link between diet and dis-ease seems to have been forgotten. The speed with which we have strayed from our more natural diet has not allowed enough time for our bodies to adapt to all the processed foods we're consuming. Though many of the people we see "know" they should eat more naturally, many don't know how to begin.

Further complicating the problem, large food manufacturers overload us with marketing hype about the health benefits of their products: high fiber, low fat, no cholesterol, reduced calories, etc. We consumers pay extra money for these overly processed foods which lack vital nutrients, do nothing to promote our health and often interfere with the healing process we need.

Doctors, too, sometimes assume their patients can't change. So instead of trying to help them eat better, exercise more and move toward a healthier lifestyle, they prescribe the newest drug being promoted to handle their symptoms.

The fast paced mentality of the 90's has displaced self-nurturing, self-caring meals prepared at home with a healing, loving spirit. Our meal plans and recipes are designed for you to use the best food available– fresh, natural and chemically free– organic if possible– to help your cells heal and to assist you in the spirit of self nurturing. Each recipe can be quickly prepared, has easy to follow directions and a pleasing taste.

After working with thousands of client's, we know the quickest way to experience measurable results from a healthy eating plan– whether it's increased speed and endurance to run a marathon, positive results on the scale, a reduction in pain from symptoms of arthritis or fibromyalgia or relief from fatigue and depression– is to focus on a natural diet. Positive results come quickest when you eat food without added chemicals, artificial colors and preservatives or refined sugars. Fast foods, highly processed, de-energized, chemically enhanced addicting foods must be avoided. Artificial, "fake foods" interfere with the healing process. They need to be replaced with fresh, natural minimally processed foods whenever possible.

As nutrition counselors and cofounders of Nutritional Weight and Wellness, we have been teaching our clients about blood sugar stabilization, the glycemic index and the importance of balancing protein, carbohydrate, and fat in their diets since the early 1980's. *Picture Book for Zone Cooks* is one more tool to help those committed to using good-tasting, natural healthy foods for self-healing.

Our goal with this book is to provide practical advice on menu planning, shopping and revising recipes to help keep you on target for Zone healing.

Living in the Zone...

1. Be realistic when setting goals. Change at a rate that is comfortable for you.

2. Be consistent. Make changes that will become a permanent part of your lifestyle.

3. Plan ahead. Being prepared with the right foods on hand (especially protein choices) helps you avoid high-risk situations– being too hungry, overly stressed, or emotionally charged– that can steer you off course.

4. Surround yourself with peers who will support your desire to change.

5. Exercise regularly if you are not already. This is also important to managing your weight, building your immune system, and balancing your hormones for the long haul.

and Loving it!

Over the past twenty years we have seen the nutritional pendulum swing from high protein to low protein and back again; from high carbohydrate to low carbohydrate and back again; and from ignoring fat, to fearing it, to praising its healing properties. During this time we have not been distracted by these dietary fads. We continued to advocate a balance between protein, carbohydrate and fat similar to the theories put forth in *The Zone*.

The foods we eat provide us with fuel in the form of calories. Calories come from carbohydrates, proteins and fats, commonly called the macronutrients. We refer to them as the building blocks of a balanced meal. Before we discuss our simple formula for combining them into a balanced meal, we'll list the best food sources of each block needed to build a strong immune system– the cornerstone of a healing diet.

PROTEIN BUILDING BLOCKS

Protein blocks for healing come from two sources:

1. Animal protein best found in:

Seafood (salmon, trout, tuna, shrimp, lobster, scallops, etc.)

Poultry, organic (chicken, turkey, game birds, etc.)

Meat, organic (beef, lamb, venison, pork, wild game, etc.)

Dairy products (milk, cheese, cottage cheese, yogurt, dairy protein powders, etc.)

Eggs (whole organic eggs, egg whites)

2. Plant protein from beans in it's most usable forms:

Tofu or soybean curd

Isolated protein powders

Textured vegetable protein

Tempeh

These protein blocks are needed by your body for energy, tissue repair, blood sugar balance and immune function. Competitive athletes and those who need to heal from a disease need more protein than others. Including protein in a meal can raise your metabolism as much as 70% above normal for up to 10 hours. What a great way for someone looking for weight loss to boost their metabolism. By feeding your body small amounts of protein throughout the day, you will keep your metabolism burning at a steady pace all day long.

Athletes, those looking for weight loss and those healing from chronic illness usually need between 75 and 100 grams of protein a day.

CARBOHYDRATE BUILDING BLOCKS

Carbohydrate blocks for healing come from four sources:

1. Fresh vegetables low on the glycemic index:

> Raw salad vegetables (leafy greens, Romaine, kale, cabbage, broccoli, cauliflower, tomato, spinach, zucchini, etc.)

> Steamed vegetables (asparagus, green beans, brussels sprouts, eggplant, turnip, etc.)

2. Fruits low on the glycemic index:

> Fresh fruits

> Frozen fruit with no sugar added (strawberries, blueberries, peaches, raspberries, etc.)

> Canned Fruit, no added sugar or in own juice (applesauce, pineapple, etc.)

3. Whole Grains and whole grain products:

> Cooked whole grains (oatmeal, amaranth, quinoa, rye, teff, wild rice, etc.)

> Whole grain rye bread

> High protein pasta made from whole grains

4. Beans and legumes lowest on the glycemic index

> Sprouted beans

> Dried (kidney, adzuki, soy, garbanzo)

> Dried legumes (lentils, black-eyed-peas, chick-peas)

> Canned beans and legumes (black beans, hummus, kidney, lentils)

> Frozen beans (sweet green soybeans, lima beans)

The best carbohydrates for healing are vegetables, vegetables, and more vegetables. Consider vegetables your main carbohydrate course, whole grain a side dish and fruit your dessert. Include a wide selection of colors, tastes and textures, both raw and steamed. Eating a variety of fruits adds interest, menu flexibility and additional antioxidants.

FAT BUILDING BLOCKS

Fat blocks for healing come from just four natural sources:

1. Unrefined, monounsaturated oils from:

> Vegetable sources (olive oil, avocado)

> Nut and seed sources (almond oil, canola oil, grape seed oil)

2. Fatty vegetables (avocados, olives)

3. Raw nuts, organic, if possible (almonds, macadamia nuts, pecans, hazelnuts, etc.)

4. Occasional fat from real dairy sources with no preservatives, (butter, cream, cream cheese, sour cream)

When we talk about fat building blocks, we are referring to the fats you add to a meal to help your body reduce insulin secretion. Monounsaturated fat is the best type to add if your goal is to burn fat. Cold-pressed, polyunsaturated fats not only provide balance, they promote healing because they are the building blocks of the good eicosanoids.

In addition to the fat you intentionally add for balance, you are also getting fat in natural foods that may be classified as protein or carbohydrate. The best sources of naturally occurring fats are found in fish, organic eggs and meats, unrefined, whole grains, leafy greens and beans such as soybeans.

BUILDING A MEAL...

The calories we receive from food usually come from a combination of macronutrients and the proportions vary greatly, but one macronutrient usually predominates. This is the one that determines if the food is classified nutritionally as a protein, carbohydrate or fat.

Understanding where proteins, carbohydrates and fats come from is the basis of our *Picture Book for Zone Cooks* primer. The next step is understanding how to put it all together simply to build balanced Zone meals.

WITH ZONE BUILDING BLOCKS

To make it easy picture the square wooden blocks you played with as a child with numbers and letters on them. Instead of containing all 26 letters of the alphabet, these blocks have only three letters: P, C and F. In place of numbers from 0 to 9 they have only three numbers: 7, 9 and 1-1/2. Each of the blocks has only one letter and one number on it: blocks with the letter P also have the number 7; blocks with the letter C have the number 9; blocks with the letter F have the number 1-1/2. The blocks with the letter P represent protein foods, blocks with the letter C are for carbohydrate foods and the ones with the letter F represent the added fats in our diet.

Empty the blocks from your pail onto the table: pick one of each to build a Zone snack; two of each for a moderate snack, light breakfast or mini meal; and three to five of each for a meal. Now you are on your way to building balanced Zone meals.

1+1+1 FORMULA=BALANCE

Our simple One+ One + One Formula is your math primer to balance each Zone meal or snack. It is based on the food blocks developed by Barry Sears in his his popular books *The Zone* and *Mastering the Zone*. To become "literate" in this way of eating, just follow our picture book of recipes. It's as easy as 1+1+1. One block of protein + one block of fat + one block of carbohydrate equals a Zone balanced meal. The ABCs (or the PFCs) of Zone literacy.

The protein blocks contain 7 grams of protein; the carbohydrate blocks contain 9 grams of carbohydrate and the fat blocks contain 1-1/2 grams of fat. Next, imagine that these blocks are spread out on your kitchen table and you are going to use them to build a balanced meal. To build a balanced Zone snack you take one protein block from the table and place it on your plate. Next add one carbohydrate block to your plate and finally a fat block. Your plate now contains one block of each: one block with the letter P, plus one block with the letter F, plus one block with the letter C. Voile, you have a Zone balanced snack. This is the **1+1+1 formula** for building a Zone snack or meal.

To determine how many protein, fat and carbohydrate building blocks you need each day refer to the charts and formulas in either *The Zone* or *Mastering The Zone*. These formulas will give you the total number of grams of protein you need each day. You divide this total by 7 to determine how many protein building blocks you need per day. Then divide this total between three meals and two snacks. Each time you eat a block of protein you balance it with a block of carbohydrate and a block of fat. You now have our 1+1+1 formula in a nutshell.

For example, if your lean body mass and activity level indicate that you need 84 grams of protein per day, that means you would need 12 building blocks of protein, 12 building blocks of fat and 12 building blocks of carbohydrate each day, divided among three meals and three snacks. An easy way to break this down would be to eat three blocks of each at breakfast, three at lunch, and three at dinner, plus three snacks of one block each (one mid-morning, one mid-afternoon and one in the evening).

So, you see, building a balanced Zone meal with these building blocks is as simple as child's play! Plus, it's fun. So stop counting calories and fat grams. Start enjoying nutritious, great tasting meals using the foods you enjoy and become healthier, slimmer and more energetic at the same time.

After you have found your protein equation, you are set to start building your meal with blocks of protein, according to your individual needs. Refer to our healing foods list in the appendix. The serving size necessary to provide you with one building block of protein has been listed there for you. To give you an idea of what a 7 gram block of immune building protein looks like here are some examples:

- 1 egg or 2 egg whites
- 1 ounce of chicken or turkey breast
- 1-1/2 ounces of fish
- 1/4 cup dry curd cottage cheese
- 3 ounces of firm tofu
- 1 ounce of tuna
- 1-1/2 ounces of 90% lean ground beef

Now, following our one + one + one formula, to build your meal, you must add one 9 gram build-ing block of carbohydrate for each block of protein you need at that meal. Remember to choose your carbohydrate blocks carefully so you have the variety and volume you need to feel satisfied. The following servings provide 9 grams of carbohydrate:

- 1 cup of cooked broccoli
- 2 cups of fresh shredded cabbage
- 4 cups of raw spinach
- 1/2 pear
- 1 cup of diced, mixed fruit
- 1/2 slice of whole grain rye bread
- 1/4 cup cooked barley

You still have one more block to add to complete your powerhouse meal. The block still missing from our one + one + one formula is the final block of fat. Volume-wise this block of fat is very small. Refer to the block worksheet we have included in the appendix to help visualize the small amount of healthy fat that is required for balance. To help you, consider these examples:

- 3 raw almonds
- 1/2 tsp. raw almond butter
- 1/3 tsp. olive oil
- 3 olives
- 1/2 tbsp. avocado
- 1 macadamia nut
- 1/2 tbsp. cream

Here is an example of how to apply this one + one + one formula to a typical meal. If you were to require 12 blocks of protein, carbohydrate and fat each day like the example we gave earlier, you may want three meals containing three block each. To build one meal your would need three blocks each of protein + carbohydrate + fat.

3+3+3 = 3 BLOCK BALANCE

You may choose to build your breakfast equation like this:

Protein block		Carbohydrate block		Fat block
1 organic egg	+	1/2 orange	+	1/3 tsp. olive oil
+		+		+
1 oz. ground turkey	+	1/2 slice rye bread	+	1/2 tbsp. tahini
+		+		+
1 oz. ground turkey	+	1/2 slice rye bread	+	1/2 tbsp. tahini
=		=		=
3 protein blocks	+	**3 carbohydrate blocks**	+	**3 fat blocks**

To prepare this breakfast, you may gently fry your egg and a two ounce lean, ground turkey patty in a non-stick skillet with 1/3 tsp. olive oil. While they are cooking, you could toast your slice of whole grain rye bread; peel and section your 1/2 orange and put it on the plate. Next, spread the one tablespoon of tahini on your toast. Place the egg, turkey patty and toast on the plate with your orange sections and sit down to enjoy a perfectly balanced meal consisting of three building blocks.

See how easy it it to get started? We will first give you examples of balanced breakfasts (enough for three weeks) built around our *Picture Book for Zone Cooks* recipes. These menu suggestions will be followed by healing breakfast recipes.

Following the breakfast recipes will be 21 snacks composed of one and two building blocks each. Our "Picture Book" snack recipes come next. Then come the lunch menus built around three blocks with the "Picture Book" recipes to support them. Finally, we provide 21 three and four block dinner menus followed by the recipes that inspired them.

We will end this book with tips for stocking a healing foods kitchen, and a shopping list to get you started.

The appendix includes our healing block food list and various worksheets our clients have found helpful. Feel free to photocopy these sheets for your own use in building your meals based on your individual healing needs.

Building Blocks to Health

• **Eat breakfast** within one hour of getting up.

• **Eat fruit** instead of fruit juice; eat vegetables instead of bread; eat small amounts of whole grains instead of processed cereals or pasta.

• **Plan your meals and snacks.** Have the foods you need on hand and eat on schedule.

• **Do not skip meals.** Eat small amounts frequently. Eat breakfast, lunch and dinner each day.

• **Eat two snacks each day.** One snack either mid-morning or mid-afternoon and one snack in the evening.

• **Combine balanced amounts** of lean protein, complex carbohydrates and healthy fats at each meal and snack.

• **Eat whole, unrefined, nutrient dense foods** as close to their natural state as possible.

• **Drink plenty of water.**

• **Read labels** to avoid preservatives and hidden carbohydrates.

• **Eat a wide variety of foods.** This will maximize your nutrient intake and minimize your chance of developing food allergies or sensitivities.

• **Listen to your body.** Customize your diet according to your unique biochemical, hormonal, nutritional and lifestyle needs.

• **Relax.** Take it easy. Be gentle with yourself.

Building Block Meals for a Balanced Day

BREAKFAST

2-4 Protein Building Blocks
2-4 Carbohydrate Building Blocks
2-4 Fat Building Blocks

OPTIONAL SNACK

1-2 Protein Building Blocks
1-2 Carbohydrate Building Blocks
1-2 Fat Building Blocks

LUNCH

2-4 Protein Building Blocks
2-4 Carbohydrate Building Blocks
2-4 Fat Building Blocks

OPTIONAL SNACK

1-2 Protein Building Blocks
1-2 Carbohydrate Building Blocks
1-2 Fat Building Blocks

DINNER

2-5 Protein Building Blocks
2-5 Carbohydrate Building Blocks
2-5 Fat Building Blocks

P.M. SNACK

1-2 Protein Building Blocks
1-2 Carbohydrate Building Blocks
1-2 Fat Building Blocks

21 Healing Breakfasts

#1— 3 blocks: 1 cup cooked steel cut oats
1/2 cup soy milk
1/2 apple, diced
2 organic eggs fried in
1 tsp. olive oil

#2— 3 blocks: 1 whole egg, plus 4 egg
whites, scrambled
2 Wasa Lite Rye Crispbread
1/2 cup honeydew, cubed
1/2 cup papaya, cubed
1 tsp. butter

#3— 4 blocks: **BREAKFAST BURRITO**
(page 15) one serving

#4— 3 blocks: **TOFU QUICHE**
(page 16) one serving
1 cup strawberries
1/4 cup blueberries
9 raw almonds, sliced

#5— 3 blocks: **TOFU SCRAMBLER**
(page 18)
1 **TURKEY BREAKFAST
SAUSAGE** *(page 19)*
1 tomato, sliced
1 cucumber, sliced
1/2 grapefruit

#6— 3 blocks: 1/2 cup cooked steel cut oats
1/4 cup cottage cheese
1/2 cup WestSoy Organic Soy Milk
1 Boca soy burger
2/3 cup raspberries
9 raw almonds

#7— 3 blocks: 3 **TURKEY NUGGETS** *(page 30)*
1 cup broccoli
1-1/2 cup cauliflower
1 cup green beans
1 tsp. butter

#8— 3 blocks: **BLUEBERRY OAT MUFFIN**
(page 20)
2 organic eggs fried in 2/3 tsp. oil
1/4 cup raspberries

#9— 3 blocks: **TOFU PUMPKIN PIE**
(page 28) 1 serving
4 soy sausage links
1/2 cup strawberries
1/2 tbsp. cream,

#10— 3 blocks: 3 **TURKEY BREAKFAST
SAUSAGES** *(page 19)*
1 slice whole grain rye toast
1/2 grapefruit, 1 tsp. butter

#11— 3 blocks: 1 oz. slice part-skim mozzarella
cheese
2 oz. sliced cold turkey breast
1 orange
2 Wasa Lite Rye crackers
1-1/2 tbsp. almond butter

#12— 3 blocks: **LEMON BAKED TURKEY
BREAST** *(page 69)* 3 oz., sliced
1/2 cup cooked quinoa
1 cup mixed fruit, diced
3 Tbsp. half and half

#13— 3 blocks: Omelet made with
      1 whole egg and 4 whites and
      1/2 cup chopped onion
      1/2 cup diced celery
      1/2 cup diced green pepper
      1/2 cup sliced mushrooms
      1/4 cup salsa, sauteed in
   1 teaspoon olive oil
   1 orange

#14— 3 blocks: 1/2 cup plain nonfat yogurt mixed
      with 1/4 cup applesauce
      1 Tbsp. protein powder
      1/2 tsp. cinnamon
      1/4 tsp. nutmeg
      vegetable glycerine to taste
   Sprinkle with 1 Tbsp. slivered
      almonds.

#15— 3 blocks: **BLUEBERRY OAT MUFFIN**
      (page 20)
   1/2 cup cottage cheese
   2 macadamia nuts,
   1 cup strawberries

#16— 3 blocks: 1 slice toasted whole grain rye
      bread topped with 3/4 cup
      cottage cheese, broil until
      cottage cheese bubbles. Top with
   1/4 cup blueberries
   9 almonds, chopped

#17— 3 blocks: 1/2 mini pita stuffed with 1/3 cup
      TOFU HUMMUS *(page 21)*
   2 oz. sliced turkey or two sliced
   hard boiled organic eggs

#18— 3 blocks: **TOFU SHAKE** *(page 22)*

#19— 3 blocks: **TOFU YOGURT**
      (page 25) 1 cup
   1 organic egg, poached
   1/2 cooked amaranth
   1 cup strawberries, sliced

#20— 3 blocks: 3 oz. chicken steamed together
      with 1/3 sweet potato
   1 cup yellow squash
   1 cup fresh green beans
   Toss with 1 tsp olive oil and herbs
      of choice

#21— 3 blocks: 3/4 cup cooked wild rice
   3 oz. cooked turkey sauteed in
      1 tsp olive oil

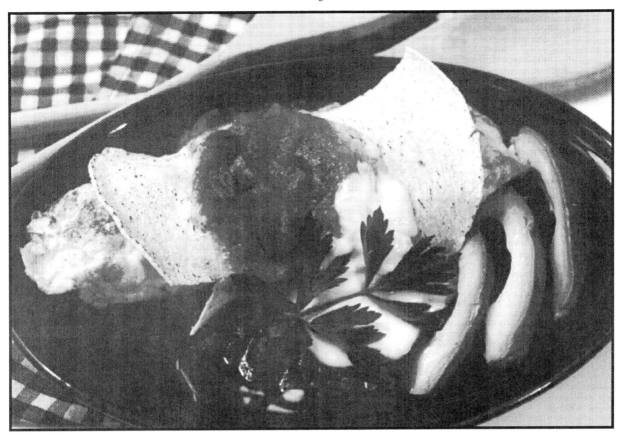

Breakfast Burritos

Ingredients:
1/3 cup potato
2 large eggs
1/4 cup dry curd cottage cheese
1 corn tortilla
1 cup low fat plain yogurt
1 tbsp. avocado
1/2 cup salsa
2/3 tsp. olive oil
salt and pepper
cayenne pepper and red pepper flakes

1. Saute in a nonstick pan:
2/3 teaspoon olive oil
1/3 cup potato - precooked, cubed or grated

2. Add and cook briefly to set:
2 large eggs - slightly beaten spices to taste

3. Add and continue to cook shaping mixture into a roll:
1/4 cup dry curd cottage cheese

4. Warm:
1 corn tortilla

5. Place egg mixture in center of warmed tortilla and top with:
1/2 cup salsa
1 tablespoon avocado
1/2 cup low fat plain yogurt

1 Serving
per serving:
4 protein blocks
4 carbohydrate blocks
4 fat blocks

Tofu Quiche

Ingredients:

1 1/3 tsp. of olive or canola oil
1 envelope Kashi
2-1/2 oz. Boca Burgers or turkey
6 large eggs (organic)
1 pound conventional tofu
3/4 cup ricotta cheese
1 cup onion
3 tbsp. lemon juice
2 tbsp. Bragg Liquid Aminos
1 tbsp. dry mustard
1/2 tsp. garlic powder
1/4 tsp. black pepper
1 egg - crust

Preheat oven to 350°

1. For crust, prepare as directed on package.

1 envelope of Kashi (beef, chicken or vegetable broth may be substituted for liquid to enhance flavor)

2. Mix in:

1 egg and press into oil sprayed 8 inch glass pie or cake pan. Bake for 20-30 minutes until mixture is firm and dry to the touch.

3. For quiche, sauté in nonstick fry pan:

1/3 teaspoon of olive or canola oil
1 cup onion - chopped
2 1/2 ounces turkey or 1 Boca burger, crumbled.

Tofu Quiche continued

4. Mix in blender and adjust seasonings to taste:
1 pound conventional tofu
6 large eggs (organic)
3/4 cup ricotta cheese
3 tablespoons lemon juice
2 tablespoons Bragg Liquid Aminos
1 tablespoon dry mustard
1/2 teaspoon garlic powder
1/4 teaspoon black pepper

5. Pour blender mixture into a bowl and stir in the following:
Saute'd Boca burger mixture and onions

6. Pour total mixture over cooked Kashi crust. Bake 45-60 minutes until firm and lightly browned. Knife inserted in center should come out clean.

✳ ***To Complete the Meal—***
serve with 1/2 cup strawberries and 1 cup steamed green beans

4 Servings
per serving:
3 protein
1 1/2 carbohydrates
3 fat

Tofu Scrambler

Ingredients:
1 large fresh egg
1 tbsp. soy milk
3 oz. conventional tofu
1/4 cup onion
1/4 cup green pepper
1 tsp. olive oil
salt and pepper

1 Serving
per serving:
2 protein blocks
1 carbohydrate block
3 fat blocks

1. Combine in bowl and beat slightly:
1 large egg
1 tablespoon soy milk
salt and pepper to taste

2. Saute in nonstick pan until tender:
1 teaspoon olive oil
1/4 cup onion - chopped
1/4 cup green pepper - chopped

3. Crumble into pan:
3 ounces conventional tofu

4. Add egg mixture to pan. Cook until firm.

❋ ***To Complete the Meal—*** *serve with 1 oz. turkey sausage or 1/4 of Baked Tofu recipe (page 77) and 1 grapefruit.*

Turkey Breakfast Sausage

Ingredients:

1-1/2 pound ground turkey (at least 90% lean)
1 tsp. salt
3/4 tsp. pepper
1-1/2 tsp. sage
1/8 tsp. red pepper flakes
1 tbsp. fennel seed

1. In a mixing bowl mix spices thoroughly into ground turkey.

2. Shape into 2-1/2 inch by 1/2 inch patties (this should yield 1 block of protein per patty)

3. Brown patties in oil sprayed fry pan until cooked through.

Yields 12 patties.

✳ ***To Complete the Meal—*** *serve 2 sausages, a poached organic egg on a slice of rye toast with 1 teaspoon butter, and 1/2 grapefruit.*

12 Servings
per serving:
1 protein
0 carbohydrates
0 fat

Blueberry Oat Muffins

Ingredients:

1 cup whole-grain wheat flour
1 cup rolled oats
1-1/2 tsp. cinnamon
1/2 tsp. baking powder
1/4 tsp. baking soda
1/2 tsp. salt
10 oz. Mori-Nu Tofu
6 tbsp. soy protein powder
1/4 cup canola oil
2 eggs
1/2 cup vegetable glycerine or fructose (if use fructose, add 1/4 cup soy milk)
1-1/2 cups fresh blueberries - or - 1-1/2 apples, chopped

1. Mix the following in a large bowl:

1 cup whole-grain wheat flour
1 cup rolled oats
1-1/2 teaspoons cinnamon
1/2 teaspoon baking powder
1/4 teaspoon baking soda
1/2 tsp. salt

2. Mix the following in a blender until smooth:

10 ounces Mori-Nu Tofu
6 tablespoons soy protein powder
1/4 cup canola oil (butter may be substituted)
2 eggs
1/2 cup vegetable glycerine or fructose (1/4 cup soy milk if fructose used)

3. Gently fold in the following:

1-1/2 cups fruit (berries or apples)

4. Fill oiled muffin tins two-thirds full. Bake at 400°, for 18-20 minutes.

Yields 1 dozen muffins.

❈ *To Complete the Meal—Serve with 1/2 cup Tofu Yogurt (page 25), 1 macadamia nut and 1/2 cup strawberries.*

12 Servings
per serving:
 1 protein block
1-1/2 carbohydrate blocks
1 fat block

Tofu Hummus

Ingredients:
15 ounces canned garbanzo beans
2 cloves garlic - minced
3 tablespoon tahini
10 ounces Mori-Nu Tofu
2 Tbsp. lemon juice
1/8 teaspoon cayenne (optional)
1 teaspoon olive oil
1-1/2 teaspoon herb salt and/or Bragg Liquid Aminos to taste
1 cup steamed broccoli - chopped (cauliflower may be substituted)

1. Combine ingredients in food processor or blender. May serve with pita bread or raw vegetables.

❋ *To Complete the Snack— serve with 1 1/2 oz. sliced turkey and 1 mini pita for a 2 block snack.*

12 Servings
per 1/2 c up serving:
1/2 protein block
1/2 carbohydrate block
2 fat blocks

Tofu Shake

Ingredients:
5 ounces (1/2 package) Mori-Nu Tofu
2 cups fresh or frozen fruit
1 cup liquid (water or soy milk)
1 scoop high protein powder (yielding 14 grams protein per scoop)
(i.e. Designer Protein, Protein Plus or Genista)
1 teaspoon oil or 9 raw almonds or 4 raw macadamia nuts (may eat or blend nuts)
4-6 ice cubes - optional

1. Combine in a blender all of the above ingredients until smooth and creamy.

---

1 Serving
per serving:
3 protein blocks
3 carbohydrate blocks
3 fat blocks

21 Healing Snacks

#1— 1 block: **TOFU YOGURT**
(page 25) 1 serving
1/2 cup blueberries
3/4 tsp. raw sunflower seeds

#2— 1-1/2 block: **TOFU SHAKE**
(page 22) 1/2 serving

#3— 2 blocks: **TOFU PAN PIZZA**
(page 52) 1/8 of pie

#4— 1 block: **TOFU GUACAMOLE
DRESSING** *(page 27)* 2 tbsp.
1 oz. sliced chicken
1/2 slice whole grain rye bread

#5— 1 block: 1/4 cup cottage cheese
2 Wasa Lite Rye crackers
3 raw almonds

#6— 1 block: 1 oz. sliced turkey
1/2 apple, sliced, 1 tbsp. tahini
spread on apple slices

#7— 2 blocks: **BLUEBERRY OAT MUFFIN**
(page 20)
1 ounce stick of string cheese
(mozzarella, part skim)
1/4 apple
3 raw almonds

#8— 1 block: 1 ounce stick of string cheese
(mozzarella, part skim)
1 cup cantaloupe

3 raw pecan halves

#9— 2 blocks: 1/2 cup plain, non-fat yogurt
1 scoop protein powder
(equal to 14 grams)
1 cup strawberries
2 macadamia nuts
Blend together in blender
Freeze in Dixie cup to eat
on the run.

#10— 2 blocks: **TOFU PUMPKIN PIE**
(page 28) 1 serving
1 TURKEY NUGGET *(page 30)*

#11— 1 block: 1 hard-boiled egg
1/2 orange
2 walnut halves

#12— 1 block: 1/4 cantaloupe
1/4 cup cottage cheese
1 Tbsp.. slivered almonds

#13— 2 blocks: 2 oz. **MUSTARD BAKED
TURKEY CUTLET** *(page 31)*
Assorted vegetables:
1/2 cup cauliflower
1/3 cup carrots
1/2 cup celery
1/2 cup broccoli
1/2 cup cucumber dipped into:
1/4 cup **TOFU CHIVE
DRESSING** *(page 26)*

#14— 2 blocks: 1/2 cup plain yogurt with
1/4 cup **BLUEBERRY FRUIT GLAZE** *(page 32)*
1/2 scoop protein powder and
6 whole hazelnuts stirred in

#15— 2 blocks: **DEVILED EGGS**
(page 33) 4 halves
1 apple, sliced

#16— 2 blocks: 1/2 cup **TOFU ONION DIP**
(page 27) served over
12 steamed asparagus spears

#17— 2 blocks: **SEASONED TURKEY CUTLET**
(page 34) 2 oz. cooked, saute´d
with 1/4 cup cooked brown rice
in 2/3 tsp. olive oil

#18— 2 blocks: 2 oz. tuna
1/2 apple, chopped, mixed with
1 Tbsp. **MAYONNAISE**
(page 35)

served on 2 Wasa crackers

#19— 1 block: **SALMON LOAF**
(page 45) 1 slice served on
1/2 slice rye bread
3 olives

#20— 2 blocks: **FISH CROQUETTES**
(page 36) 2
1/2 cup sliced zucchini,
1/2 cup cherry tomatoes,
1 green pepper, sliced,
1 cup cauliflower, dipped in
1/4 cup **TOFU MAYONNAISE**
(page 27)

#21— 1 block: 3/4 cup Eden Soy milk
3 almonds

Tofu Yogurt

Ingredients:
10 ounces Mori-Nu Tofu
2 tablespoons vegetable glycerine (or to taste)
1/4 teaspoon vanilla
1/4 teaspoon salt

1. Mix all of the above ingredients in blender until smooth.

Can be used in any recipe calling for yogurt.

❋ *To Complete the Snack—add 1 cup diced strawberries and 3 raw almonds.*

3 Servings
per 1/2 cup serving:
1 protein block
0 carbohydrate blocks
0 fat blocks

Tofu Chive Dressing (TOP)

Ingredients:
10 oz. Mori-Nu Light Tofu
2 tbsp. oil (olive, flax or canola oil)
2 tbsp. vinegar
1 tbsp. Bragg Liquid Aminos
1 tsp. salt
1/2 tsp. garlic powder or minced garlic
1/4 tsp. fresh ground black pepper
1/2 cup fresh chives - chopped

1. Blend in food processor the following ingredients until smooth and adjust seasonings to taste:
10 ounces tofu
2 tablespoons oil
2 tablespoons vinegar
1 tablespoon Braggs
1/2 teaspoon minced garlic or powder
1 teaspoon salt
1/4 teaspoon fresh ground pepper

2. Fold in:
1/2 cup fresh chives - chopped

3. Refrigerate overnight

❋ ***To Complete the Meal—*** *serve with 2 1/2 oz. tuna on mixed greens and vegetables with 1 Wasa cracker for a 3 block meal.*

6 Servings
per 1/3 cup serving:
1/2 protein blocks
0 carbohydrate blocks
3 fat blocks

Tofu Guacamole Dressing (BOTTOM)

Ingredients:
10 oz. Mori-Nu Tofu
1 avocado
3 tbsp. Mayonnaise
dash Bragg Liquid Aminos
dash Paprika and chili pow-
der
1 clove garlic
1/2 tsp. salt

1. Mash the following ingre-dients together:
10 ounces tofu
1 avocado - peeled

2. Add ingredients, blend and adjust to taste:
3 tablespoons mayonnaise
(with 3 grams of fat per
tablespoon)
2 tablespoons lemon juice
1 clove garlic - minced

1/2 teaspoon salt
dash of each: Paprika and
chili powder
dash of Bragg Liquid Aminos

8 Servings
per 1/4 cup serving:
0 protein blocks
0 carbohydrate blocks
3 fat blocks

Onion Tofu Dip (LEFT)

Ingredients:
10 ounces Mori-Nu Tofu
2 Tbsp. olive oil
2 tbsp. fresh lemon juice
1 tbsp. instant vegetable
bouillon (Health food brand)
1/3 cup dried onions
1 clove garlic
1 tsp salt - optional

1. Blend the following ingredients in food proces-sor or blender until creamy smooth:
10 ounces tofu
2 tablespoons olive oil
2 tablespoons fresh lemon juice

1. Stir in the following and adjust seasonings to taste:
1/3 cup dried onions
1 tablespoon instant veg-etable bouillon
1 clove garlic - minced

1. Refrigerate overnight to blend flavors.

❋ **To Complete the Snack—**
stir 1 oz. tuna, crab, shrimp or chicken into dip and serve 1 1/2 cups broccoli and cau-liflower florettes for dipping for a 2 block snack.

3 Servings
per 2/3 cup serving:
1 protein blocks
1 carbohydrate blocks
2 fat blocks

Tofu Mayo (RIGHT)

Ingredients:
10 ounces Mori-Nu Tofu
2 Tbsp. olive, flax or canola oil
1-2 tbsp.vinegar
1/4 tsp. salt
1 tsp. sugar

1. Blend in food processor or blender all of the above until smooth and creamy.

2. Chill at least 1 hour for flavors to blend.

6 Servings
per serving:
1/2 protein blocks
0 carbohydrate blocks
3 fat blocks

Tofu Pumpkin Pie

Ingredients:

15 oz. Mori-Nu Lite Tofu
1/2 cup Wasa Crisp Bread (Lite rye)
2 cups canned pumpkin - unsweetened
1 scoop protein powder
1/4 cup vegetable glycerine
1/4 cup pure maple syrup
1 tsp. vanilla
1 egg
2 tbsp. butter
1 apple
1 egg
1 tbsp. vegetable glycerine
dash cinnamon
1/2 tsp. salt
1 tsp. cinnamon
1/4 tsp. cloves
1/4 tsp. nutmeg
1/4 tsp. ginger

Preheat oven to 350

1. Crust—
Mix following and press into oil sprayed 8" pie pan:
1/2 cup Wasa Crackers - crushed (8 crackers)
dash cinnamon
2 tablespoons butter - melted
1 apple - grated
1 egg - beaten
1 tablespoon vegetable glycerine

2. Bake 20 minutes. Cool.

3. Filling—
Blend in food processor or blender until smooth:
15 ounces Mori-Nu Lite Tofu

4. Add and blend well:
1/4 cup vegetable glycerine
1/4 cup pure maple syrup
2 cups canned pumpkin - unsweetened
1 scoop protein powder (15 grams or more per serving)
1 teaspoon vanilla
1 egg
1/2 teaspoon salt

Tofu Pumpkin Pie Continued

May double the following seasonings for more spicy pie:

1 teaspoon cinnamon
1/4 teaspoon cloves
1/4 teaspoon nutmeg
1/4 teaspoon ginger

5. Bake 35-40 minutes. Chill. (Filling will firm as it chills).

❋ ***To Complete the Snack—*** *add 1 oz. sliced turkey for a 2 block snack.*

---

8 Servings
per serving:
1 protein block
2-1/2 carbohydrate blocks
2 fat blocks

Turkey Nuggets

Ingredients:
16 oz. turkey breast
4 Wasa Lite Rye Crackers
1 tsp. poultry seasoning
2 tbsp. fresh parsley

16 Servings
per serving:
1 protein blocks
0 carbohydrate blocks
0 fat blocks

Preheat oven to 350°.

1. Crush and set aside:
4 Wasa Lite Rye Crackers

2. Mix with crushed crackers:
1 teaspoon poultry seasoning
2 tablespoon fresh parsley

3. Cut into 16 "nuggets":
16 ounces turkey breast

4. Coat turkey nuggets with cracker mixture.

5. Bake on oil sprayed cooking sheet for 30 minutes turning once.

✳ ***To Complete the Snack—***
Serve with 1/2 apple and 3 raw almonds.

Mustard Baked Turkey Cutlet

Ingredients:

8 oz. turkey tenderloin
1/2 cup prepared yellow mustard
1/2 tsp. black pepper
1/2 tsp. basil leaves
2 tsp. parsley - dried

4 Servings

per serving:
2 protein blocks
0 carbohydrate blocks
0 fat blocks

Preheat oven to 325°.

1. Place in oil sprayed baking dish:
8 ounces turkey tenderloin

2. Combine the following and spread on turkey:
1/2 cup prepared yellow mustard
2 teaspoons parsley - dried
1/2 teaspoon black pepper
1/2 teaspoon basil leaves - dried

3. Seal tightly with aluminum foil.

4. Bake at 325° for 1 hour.

✳ ***To Complete the Snack—*** *serve with 2 Ryvita sesame crisp bread and 2 cups raw, mixed vegetable sticks—jicama, celery, cucumber, zucchini, carrots, etc.*

Blueberry Fruit Glaze

Ingredients:

1 cup blueberries - fresh or frozen
1 tbsp. cornstarch
1/4 cup lemon juice
2 tbsp. vegetable glycerine or fructose

---

2 Servings

per 1/2 cup serving:
0 protein blocks
1 carbohydrate block
0 fat blocks

---

1. In saucepan, warm over low heat:
1 cup blueberries - fresh or frozen

2. Combine in small bowl:
1 tablespoon corn starch (arrowroot may be substituted)
1/4 cup lemon juice
2 tablespoons vegetable glycerine or crystalline fructose

3. Gently stir lemon mixture into fruit. Heat until thickened.

✳ ***To Complete the Snack—*** *stir Blueberry Fruit Glaze and protein powder (equal to 7 grams of protein) into 1/2 cup plain fat free yogurt and top with 6 chopped almonds.*

Deviled Eggs

Ingredients:

6 organic hard-boiled eggs
3 tbsp. reduced fat mayon-
naise (3 grams per tbsp.)
1 tsp. vinegar
1/2 tsp. salt
dash white pepper
1/4 tsp. paprika
1/2 tsp. dry mustard

1. Cut hard-boiled eggs in half lengthwise, remove yolks and mash with:

1 teaspoon vinegar
1/2 teaspoon salt
dash of white pepper
1/4 teaspoon paprika
1/2 teaspoon dry mustard

2. Refill egg whites and refrigerate.

✿ ***To complete the Snack—*** *serve with 2 Wasa Crackers or 2 cups raw mixed vegetables.*

6 Servings
2 halves per serving:
1 protein blocks
0 carbohydrate blocks
1 fat blocks

Seasoned Turkey Cutlet

Ingredients:

1 lb. turkey tenderloin
2 tbsp. Hain Canola Italian dressing
1 bunch fresh parsley - chopped
1/4 cup fresh Italian mixed herbs

8 Servings

per serving:
2 protein blocks
0 carbohydrate blocks
1/2 fat block

Preheat oven to 325°.

1. Coat baking pan with olive oil spray.

2. Center on prepared pan:
1 pound turkey breast cutlet

3. With pastry brush, coat top and sides with:
Hain Canola Italian dressing

4. Coat with:
Chopped parsley
1/4 cup fresh Italian herbs

5. Bake at 325° for one hour.

6. Slice into 8 two ounce slices or 16 one ounce slices.

✪ *To Complete the Meal— serve 3 ounces of cutlet with Zucchini Medley (page 64) and 1/2 orange, sectioned.*

Mayonnaise

Ingredients:

1 egg, raw, pasteurized
3/4 cup cold-pressed oil
1/8 tsp. dry mustard
1/8 tsp. white pepper
2 tbsp. fresh lemon juice
paprika
salt
onion and garlic powder

1. Blend in blender on high for 5 seconds:

1 egg
1/8 teaspoon dry mustard
1/8 teaspoon white pepper
2 tablespoons fresh lemon juice
dash paprika
pinch of salt
onion and garlic powder - to taste

2. With blender running at high speed, very slowly drizzle in a thin stream until mixture becomes white and oil is completely blended in:

3/4 cup cold-pressed oil

3. Refrigerate in tightly sealed container.

8 Servings
per 2 tbsp. serving:
0 protein blocks
0 carbohydrate blocks
3 fat blocks

Fish Croquettes

Ingredients:

6 oz. canned tuna, salmon or trout
1 egg
4 Wasa Crisp Bread (Lite Rye)
4 tbsp. onion
1 tsp. dried celery flakes
onion and/or garlic powder
1/8 tsp. powdered mustard (optional)

3 Servings

per serving:
2 protein blocks
1/2 carbohydrate block
0 fat blocks

Preheat oven to 300°.

1. Mix the following ingredients gently with a fork:

6 ounces fish, drained
1 egg - slightly beaten
4 Wasa crackers - crushed
4 tablespoons onion - finely chopped
1 teaspoon dried celery flakes
1/8 teaspoon powdered mustard (optional)
dash onion and/or garlic powder

2. Shape into 9 croquettes. Bake at 300° up to 5 minutes on a side until evenly browned on all sides.

✳ ***To Complete the Meal—*** *sauté 1/4 cup cooked acorn squash, 1/2 cup onion, 3/4 cup red pepper and 1/4 cup cooked quinoa in 1 teaspoon olive oil. Serve with 4 fish croquettes for a 3 block meal.*

21 Healing Lunches

1/3 tsp. butter

#1— 3 blocks: **CURRIED CHICKEN CUCUMBER SALAD**
(page 39) one serving
2 Wasa crackers
1/2 mango

#8— 3 blocks: **3 FISH CROQUETTES**
(page 36)
2 cups spinach tossed with
  1 diced tomato
  1 cup sliced mushrooms
  1 tsp. oil with vinegar and herbs
  for dressing
1 kiwi fruit

#2— 3 blocks: **LENTIL SALAD** *(page 40)*
served on fresh romaine
lettuce leaf

#9— 3 blocks: **TROUT SALAD SUPREME**
(page 47)
served on lettuce leaves

#3— 3 blocks: **SPAGHETTI PIE**
(page 41) 1 serving

#10— 3 blocks: **TURKEY QUINOA SALAD**
(page 48)
serve on large fresh lettuce leaf

#4— 3 blocks: **QUINOA VEGETABLE STEW**
(page 42)

#11— 3 blocks: **TOFU POTATO SOUP**
(page 49) 1 serving
2 oz. sliced chicken
1 kiwi fruit

#5— 3 blocks: **TOFU EGG SALAD**
(page 43) 1 serving
1 tomato, sliced
2 cup mixed salad greens
2 tsp. **HEALTHY SALAD DRESSING** *(page 44)*

#12— 3 blocks: **SOUTHWESTERN CHILI**
(page 50) 1 serving
1/2 apple
2 cups salad greens

#6— 3 blocks: **SALMON LOAF** *(page 45)*
1 slice whole grain rye bread
mustard

#13— 4 blocks: **TUNA STUFFED TOMATOES**
(page 51) 1 serving
2 cups raw bite sized vegetables

#7— 4 blocks: **TEX/MEX TURKEY SALAD**
(page 46)
1 small baked potato

2 Ryvita crackers

#14— 3 blocks: **TOFU PAN PIZZA**
(*page 52*) 1 serving

#15— 3 blocks: **SALMON SALAD SUPREME**
(*page 54*) 1 serving
1 oz. cheese
1/2 orange

#16— 3 blocks: **TOFU CHEESECAKE**
(*Page 55*) 1 serving
1 oz. sliced cheese or
1/2 cup **TOFU YOGURT**
(*page 25*)
1/2 cup **BLUEBERRY FRUIT
GLAZE** (*page 32*)

#17— 3 blocks: **TOFU CAULIFLOWER EGG
SALAD** (*page 56*) 1 serving

2 cups mixed greens
12 grapes

#18— 3 blocks: **SEASONED TURKEY CUTLET**
(*page 34*) 3 oz.
ZUCCHINI MEDLEY (*page 64*)

#19— 3 blocks: **BLUEBERRY SMOOTHIE**
(*page 57*) 1 serving
1/2 cup cottage cheese
9 raw almonds

#20— 4 blocks: **FRESH TUNA KABOBS**
(*page 58*) 1 serving
1/2 cup fresh strawberries

#21— 4 blocks: **ITALIAN STYLE TURKEY
BREAST** (*page 63*) 1 serving
served over 3/4 cup cooked
spelt sauteed in 1-1/2 tsp.

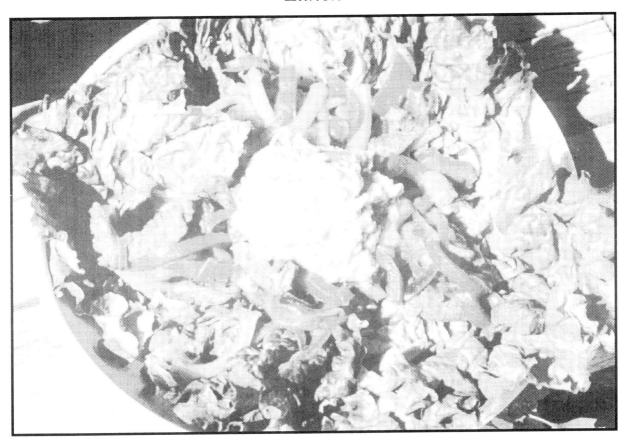

Curried Chicken Cucumber Salad

Ingredients:
8 oz. chicken breast strips
2/3 tsp. extra-virgin olive oil
3 tsp. curry powder
dash salt and pepper
1/2 cup onion
2 cups cucumber
1 red bell pepper
1 green bell pepper

1. Heat in skillet:
2/3 teaspoon olive oil

2. to hot oil add:
2 tsp. curry powder (or to taste)

3. Hold pan off heat and "swirl in":
8 oz chicken breast strips
1/2 cup onion - diced

4. Reduce heat, add and cook 2 to 3 minutes, just until heated through:
2 cups cucumber - diced
1 red bell pepper, sliced into strips
1 green bell pepper, sliced into strips

❊ ***To Complete the Meal—***
arrange 6 cups romaine on two plates, spoon 1/2 hot chicken salad over greens, scoop 1/4 cup Tofu Guacamole Dressing (page 00) onto center of salad and serve.

---

2 Servings

per serving:
4 protein blocks
1 carbohydrate blocks
1 fat blocks

Lentil Salad

Ingredients:
1 cup lentils
1 bay leaf
1 medium onion
1/2 cup green pepper
1/2 cup red bell pepper
1 cup fresh tomato
1/2 cup onion
6 ounces cooked turkey
2 tbsp. olive oil
2 tbsp. lemon juice
salt and pepper

---

2 Servings
per serving:
3 protein blocks
3 carbohydrate blocks
3 fat blocks

---

1. In 2 quart sauce pan, bring 4 cups of water to boil and add:
1 cup lentils
1 bay leaf
1 medium onion - peeled with 3 whole cloves inserted

2. Reduce heat, cover and simmer until lentils are firm but tender. Drain and rinse with cold water. Discard bay leaf and onion. Allow lentils to cool.

3. In large bowl, combine lentils with:
1 cup of cooked and cooled lentils

1/2 cup onion - diced
1/2 cup green pepper - diced
1/2 cup red bell pepper - diced
1 cup fresh tomato - diced
6 ounces cooked turkey
2 teaspoons olive oil
2 tablespoons lemon juice
salt and pepper to taste

4. Marinate for one hour - overnight is best. Serve on lettuce leaves.

Spaghetti Pie

Ingredients:

1 pound ground turkey (chicken, veal or lean ground beef may be substituted).
2 cups fresh tomato
4 large organic eggs
1/8 tsp. cayenne pepper
1 tsp. salt
6 oz. spaghetti
2 tbsp. olive oil
1 cup onion
1 clove garlic
2 tbsp. fresh chopped mixed italian seasonings

Preheat oven to 375°.

1. Combine the following in mixing bowl and gently stir:
4 large eggs
1/8 teaspoon cayenne pepper to taste
1/2 teaspoon salt
6 ounces pasta - cooked as directed

2. Pour above mixture into oil sprayed 9 inch pie plate and press against sides and bottom to form a crust.

3. Brown in skillet:
2 tablespoons olive oil
1 cup onion- chopped
1 clove garlic - minced
1 pound ground meat
1/2 teaspoon salt

4. Remove from heat and add:
2 cups fresh tomato - chopped

5. Pour mixture into spaghetti and bake 30 minutes.

6 Servings
per serving:
3 protein blocks
3 carbohydrate blocks
3 fat blocks

Quinoa Vegetable Stew

Ingredients:

1 cup quinoa
2 tbsp. olive oil
1 pound ground turkey
1-1/2 cups leeks
1/2 cup carrot
1/2 cup zucchini
1/2 cup celery
1/2 green pepper
1/2 cup red pepper
1/2 cup fresh tomato
1/2 cup cilantro
1 tbsp. dried oregano leaves
1 tbsp. dried basil leaves
2 tbsp. chili powder
7 cups water (or broth)
2 tbsp. seasoned vegetable salt
1 bay leaf
1/2 cup fresh green beans
2 tbsp. Bragg Liquid Aminos lime juice

1. Brown in dry kettle until toasty:

1 cup quinoa, rinsed and drained

2. Add and cook until soft:

2 tablespoons olive oil
1 pound ground turkey
1-1/2 cups leeks - diced
1/2 cup carrot - diced
1/2 cup zucchini - diced
1/2 cup celery - diced
1/2 green pepper - diced
1/2 cup red pepper - diced
1/2 cup fresh tomato - diced
1/2 cup cilantro - minced
1 tablespoon dried oregano leaves
1 tablespoon dried basil leaves
2 tablespoons chili powder

3. Add and bring to boil - reduce heat and simmer for 20-25 minutes until quinoa is cooked:

7 cups water (or broth)
2 teaspoons seasoned vegetable salt
1 bay leaf

4. Add and simmer for an additional 5 minutes:

1/2 cup fresh green beans
2 tablespoons Bragg Liquid Aminos

Serve with a dash of lime juice

6 Servings

per serving:
3 protein blocks
3 carbohydrate blocks
3 fat blocks

Tofu Egg Salad

Ingredients:

*1 pound conventional tofu
(freeze overnight, and thaw
prior to using)
1 tbsp. yellow mustard
1/4 tsp. tumeric
1/2 tsp. salt
1/4 tsp. black pepper
1 cup celery
1/4 cup green onions
3 tbsp. mayonnaise (with 3
fat grams fat per tbsp.)*

**1. Thaw frozen tofu and
drain water from block by
placing in dish towel and
squeezing liquid. Crumble
tofu and mix the following
in a bowl:**

*1 tablespoon yellow mustard
1/4 teaspoon tumeric
1/2 teaspoon salt
1/4 teaspoon black pepper
1 cup celery - diced
1/4 cup green onions -
minced
3 tablespoons mayonnaise*

❊ *To Complete the Meal—*
serve in 1 mini pita.

2 Servings
per serving:
3 protein blocks
1 carbohydrate block
3 fat blocks

Healthy Salad Dressing

Ingredients:

1/2 cup fresh lemon juice
1/2 cup extra virgin unrefined olive oil (or other cold-pressed oil)
1 clove garlic
oregano, thyme, basil, parsley, dill cayenne, sea salt, tar-

1. Shake in an opaque container with tight-fitting lid:

1/2 cup lemon juice
1/2 cup olive oil (or alternative oil)
1 clove garlic - minced

2. Add any of the following seasonings to taste:

oregano, thyme, basil, parsley, dill, cayenne, sea salt, tarragon

3. Refrigerate several hours to allow flavors to blend.

16 Servings
per 2 teaspoon serving:
0 protein blocks
0 carbohydrate blocks
3 fat blocks

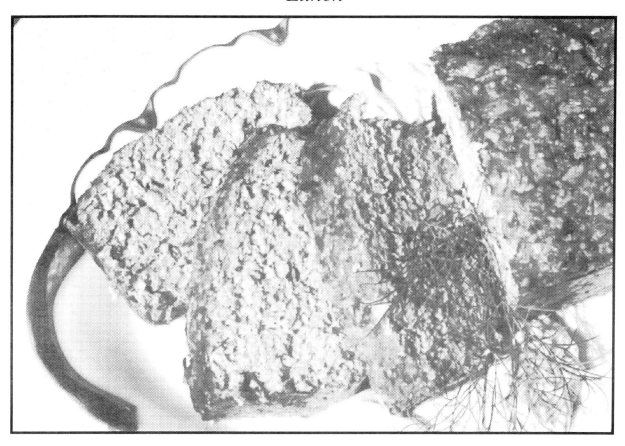

Salmon Loaf

Ingredients:

1-1/2 cups salmon - canned
1 cup oats - steal cut
1 tsp. salt
1 tsp. black pepper
1 cup soy milk
2 organic eggs
2 tbsp. butter
1/2 cup green pepper
1/2 cup onion

5 Servings

per serving:
3 protein blocks
2 carbohydrate blocks
3 fat blocks

Preheat oven to 350.

1. Mix well and let stand while sauteing vegetables:
1-1/2 cups salmon - (drained and cleaned)
1 cup oats
1 teaspoon salt
1 teaspoon pepper
1 cup soy milk
2 eggs - lightly beaten

2. Saute until tender:
2 tablespoons butter
1/2 cup green pepper - diced
1/2 cup onion - diced

3. Mix vegetables with salmon mixture. Place mixture in an oil sprayed 8" loaf pan. Bake 40 minutes until golden brown.

❋ ***To Complete the Meal—*** *serve a large green salad or 2 cups green vegetables.*

Tex/Mex Turkey Salad

Ingredients:
2 tsp. olive oil
6 ounces turkey breast (skin-less)
1 head romaine (or dark leafy green lettuce)
1/2 cup salsa
1 tsp. chili powder (ancho and guajillo chili powder may be used)
1/2 tsp. paprika
dash of salt and pepper
onion and garlic powder to taste

1. Heat in skillet.
2 teaspoons olive oil

2. Add the following and brown in skillet turning meat until pieces are coated.
6 ounces turkey breast (cut into 1/2" cubes)
dash salt and pepper
1 teaspoon chili powder
1/2 teaspoon paprika
onion and garlic powder to taste

3. Cover skillet and continue cooking until meat is done.

4. Divide the following into two portions and arrange on dinner plates:
1 head romaine lettuce

5. Spoon half of turkey mixture over each plate of greens. Divide and pour on each serving:
1/2 cup salsa

❋ *To Complete the Meal— serve with 1 orange.*

2 Servings
per serving:
3 protein blocks
1 carbohydrate blocks
3 fat blocks

Trout Salad Supreme

Ingredients:

1 can Rainbow Trout (drain if desired)
3 hard-boiled eggs
1-1/2 cups apples (with peel)
4 tbsp. mayonnaise (with 3 grams fat per tbsp.)
1-1/2 cups celery
1 tbsp. lemon juice
dash of each: salt and onion salt

1. Mix all of the ingredients in a large bowl. Serve on bed of lettuce or kale.

3 Servings
per serving:
3 protein blocks
3 carbohydrate blocks
3 fat blocks

Turkey Quinoa Salad

Ingredients:

1/2 cup quinoa
1 cup water
3/4 pound cooked turkey breast
1/4 cup green onion
1 tbsp. olive oil
1/4 cup lemon juice
fresh basil and curry powder
4 lettuce leaves

3 Servings
per serving:
3 protein blocks
3 carbohydrate blocks
3 fat blocks

1. Rinse well, then drain quinoa. Combine in 2 quart saucepan, bring to boil then simmer uncovered for 15-20 minutes or until all the water is absorbed:
1/2 cup quinoa
1 cup water

2. Combine cooled quinoa in large bowl with:
3/4 pound turkey breast
1/4 cup green onion - chopped
1 tablespoon olive oil
1/4 cup lemon juice

fresh basil - chopped - to taste
curry powder to taste

3. Refrigerate for 1-2 hours to allow blending of flavors. When ready to serve, divide mixture and spoon onto:
4 leaves of lettuce for garnish

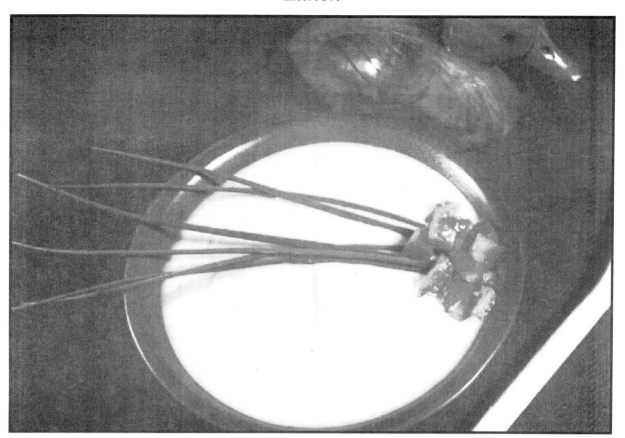

Tofu Potato Soup

Ingredients:
4 cups chicken broth
1-1/2 pounds sweet potatoes - (white potatoes may be used)
1 cup onion
10 ounces Mori-Nu Tofu
2 tbsp. olive oil
1/2 tsp. salt

6 Servings
per 1 1/2 cup serving:
1 protein block
2-1/2 carbohydrate blocks
3 fat blocks

1. In 3-quart sauce pan, simmer:
4 cups chicken broth
1-1/2 pounds sweet potatoes - peeled and cubed
1 cup onion - diced
1/2 teaspoon salt

2. While above is simmering, combine in blender or food processor and set aside:
10 ounces Mori-Nu Tofu
2 tablespoons olive oil

3. When potato mixture is cooked, drain and reserve liquid. Puree potato mixture in blender (depending on capacity of blender, this process will have to be repeated several times). If too thick, thin with 1/2 cup soy milk.

4. Pour blended mixture into the reserved broth. Adjust seasonings to taste.

5. Prior to serving, add 1/4 teaspoon pepper.

✳ *To Complete the Meal— serve with 2/3 cup Tofu Egg Salad (page 43) on a large lettuce leaf and 1 Wasa cracker.*

Southwestern Chili

Ingredients:
2 tsp. olive oil
1/2 pound lean ground turkey
1 cup onion
1 cup green pepper
2 cups Roma tomatoes
1/2 tsp. paprika
1 tsp. chili powder
garlic, salt and pepper to taste

---

2 Servings
per serving:
3 Protein blocks
1-1/2 carbohydrate blocks
3 fat blocks

---

1. In 2 quart sauce pan, brown together:
2 teaspoons olive oil
1/2 pound ground turkey

3. Add and cook for an additional 3 minutes:
1 cup onion - chopped

4. Add the remaining vegetables and spices and cook until tender:
1 cup green pepper - cut in 1" pieces
2 cups Roma tomatoes - chopped

1/2 teaspoon paprika
1 teaspoon chili power (for authentic southwestern taste, use ancho and guajillo chili powder)
garlic, salt and pepper to taste

❋ ***To Complete the Meal—***
Serve with 1 Wasa cracker and 1 kiwi fruit.

Tuna-Stuffed Tomatoes

Ingredients:

2 large romaine lettuce leaves
2 large tomatoes
6 ounces water-packed tuna-drained
2 hard-boiled eggs
1/2 cup celery
1 green onion
3 tbsp. mayonnaise (with 3 grams fat per tbsp.)

2 Servings

per serving:
4 protein blocks
1-1/2 carbohydrate blocks
4 fat blocks

1. Combine in a bowl:
6 ounces water-packed tuna - drained
2 hard-boiled eggs - diced
1/2 cup celery - finely chopped
1 green onion - finely chopped
3 tablespoons mayonnaise

2. Add seasonings to taste:
garlic powder, chopped fresh basil and dill

3. Prepare tomato "blossoms" by making 4-6 cuts from center to bottom. Pull "petals" away from center.
2 large fresh tomatoes - chopped

4. Place lettuce leave on each plate, top with tomato "blossom". Divide tuna mixture evenly and spoon onto center of each tomato.

5. Top each with:
3 almonds - finely chopped

❊ ***To Complete the Meal—*** *serve with one Wasa cracker and 1 cup blueberries.*

Tofu Pan Pizza

Ingredients:
3/4 cup whole-grain wheat flour
1 tsp. baking powder
1 cup tomato sauce
2 cups fresh tomatoes
1/2 tsp. salt
1 tsp. Italian seasoning
8 oz. mozzarella cheese, part skim milk
3 oz. cooked chicken breast
1 tsp. olive oil
8 oz. conventional tofu
1 egg
2 tsp. olive oil- crust
1 cup onion
1 cup green pepper
2 cloves garlic
1/2 tsp. salt

Preheat oven to 400°.

1. For sauce, sauté in skillet:
1 teaspoon olive oil
1 cup onion - chopped
1 cup green pepper - chopped
2 cloves garlic - minced

2. Add the following, bring to boil and simmer 20-30 minutes until thick.
1 cup tomato sauce
2 cups fresh tomatoes - chopped
1/2 teaspoon salt
1 teaspoon Italian seasoning (or 1/2 tsp. each, fresh oregano and basil)

3. While sauce is cooking, prepare crust.
8 ounces conventional tofu
1 egg
2 teaspoons olive oil
1/2 teaspoon salt

4. Add and blend again:
3/4 cup whole-grain wheat flour
1 teaspoon baking powder

Tofu Pan Pizza continued

5. Spread dough out on a 12" oil sprayed pizza or baking sheet. Spoon sauce onto dough. Top with:
8 ounces mozzarella cheese
3 ounces chicken breast - cook, cubed

6. Bake at 400° for 30 minutes.

4 Servings
per serving:
3-1/2 protein blocks
3 carbohydrate blocks
3 fat blocks

Adding Herbs and Spices

Herbs and spices can create magic in the kitchen. Adding fresh chopped herbs to meals that are being re-warmed imparts wonderful flavor. You can purchase dried herbs from the store, but growing your own is immensely satisfying. Fresh herbs have so much more flavor than dried ones and people sensitive to molds need to be very careful of dried herbs. It is convenient to buy fresh herbs in the produce section of the grocery store these days and fresh herb combinations are often packaged together, such as basil, oregano and thyme or rosemary, tarragon and dill for adding zest to tomato sauce, salad dressings or salads.

Herbs	dill	rosemary	dried peppers
basil	fennel	tarragon	garlic powder
bay leaves	marjoram	**Spices**	fresh ginger root
caraway seeds	mustard powder	allspice	ginger
cayenne pepper	oregano	cardamom	mace
celery seeds	paprika	cinnamon	nutmeg
chili powder	parsley	cloves	onion powder
coriander	red pepper flakes	curry	tumeric
cumin	sage		

Salmon Salad Supreme

Ingredients:

1 7.5 oz. can water-packed salmon, drained
1/2 cup celery - diced
2 tbsp. green onion
1/2 cup frozen peas
1 hard-boiled egg
5 large ripe olives
2 tbsp. mayonnaise (with 3 grams fat per tbsp.)
2 tsp. dried basil leaves

1. Combine in a large bowl:

1 can of water-packed salmon, drained
1/2 cup celery - diced
2 tablespoons green onion - chopped
1/2 cup frozen peas
1 hard-boiled egg - peeled and chopped
5 large ripe olives - sliced
2 tablespoons mayonnaise (with 3 grams fat per tbsp.)
2 teaspoons dried basil leaves

2. Divide into 2 portions and place on top:

2 large lettuce leaves

✳ ***To Complete the Meal—***
Serve with 2 Wasa Crackers or 2 cups tossed salad.

2 Servings

per serving:
3 protein blocks
2 carbohydrate blocks
3 fat blocks

Tofu Cheesecake

Ingredients:

28 oz. conventional tofu
1/2 cup vegetable glycerine
5 tbsp. lemon juice
2 tbsp. arrowroot
2 tsp. vanilla
1/2 tsp. salt
3/4 cup oat flour
2 tbsp. brown sugar
2 tbsp. butter
pinch cinnamon

---

8 Servings

per serving:
1 protein blocks
2 carbohydrate blocks
3 fat blocks

Preheat oven to 325°.

**1. Prepare crust—
Combine the following in a small bowl and mix until a fluffy crumb is formed:**
3/4 cup oat flour
2 tablespoons brown sugar
2 tablespoons butter
pinch cinnamon

2. Press into 8" pie or cake pan. Bake 10-12 minutes until golden brown. Cool.

**3. Prepare filling—
Puree in a blender in batches until smooth:**
28 ounces conventional tofu
1/2 cup vegetable glycerine
5 tablespoons lemon juice
2 tablespoons arrowroot
2 teaspoons vanilla
1/2 teaspoon salt

4. Pour into cooled crust spreading evenly. Bake 45-50 minutes until center is set. Let cool. Refrigerate for 2 or more hours. Serve chilled with fresh fruit or fruit glaze *(page ?)*.

❋ *To Complete the Meal—
serve with 2 ounces turkey in 1/2 pita bread.*

Tofu Cauliflower Egg Salad

Ingredients:

10 ounces Mori-Nu Tofu or conventional tofu
3 hard boiled eggs
2 tbsp. green onion
1/4 cup green pepper
1/2 cup celery
1 cup cauliflower florettes
3 tbsp. mayonnaise (with 3 grams fat per tbsp.)
1 tsp. dry mustard
1/2 tsp. garlic powder
1/4 tsp. dill weed
3 tsp. lemon juice

1. In large bowl cube into 1/2" squares:
10 ounces Mori-Nu Tofu or conventional tofu

2. Add:
3 hard boiled eggs - chopped
2 tablespoons green onion - diced
1/4 cup green pepper - diced
1/2 cup celery - diced
1 cup cauliflower florettes

2 Servings
per serving:
3 protein blocks
1 carbohydrate blocks
3 fat blocks

3. Combine and gently stir into vegetables:
3 tablespoons mayonnaise
1 teaspoon dry mustard
1/2 teaspoon garlic powder
1/4 teaspoon dill weed
3 teaspoon lemon juice

4. Chill at least 1 hour prior to serving (necessary for flavors to blend).

❈ *To Complete the Meal—serve with 2 Wasa crackers and 1/2 apple.*

Blueberry Smoothie

Ingredients:

1-1/2 cups blueberries
1 banana - frozen
10 oz. Mori-Nu Tofu
2 tbsp. maple syrup (pure) or
may use 1 tbsp. of vegetable
glycerine or 1 tbsp. fructose
1/4 tsp. almond extract
1 cup soy milk
(May need to add up to 4 ice
cubes if using a fresh
banana)

1. Combine the above ingredients in blender and puree until smooth.

✼ *To Complete the Meal—* *serve with 4 Deviled Egg halves (page 33).*

3 Servings
per serving:
1 protein blocks
3 carbohydrate blocks
0 fat blocks

Fresh Tuna Kabobs

Ingredients:
1 1/4 pound yellow fin tuna
1 spaghetti squash (3 lbs.)
8 large mushroom caps
1 cup zucchini
1/2 cup sweet red pepper
1/2 cup onion
2 tbsp. fresh parsley
2 tsp. butter
1/4 cup white wine vinegar
2 tbsp. green onions
2 tbsp. lime juice
2 tsp. olive oil
1 tbsp. dijon mustard
1/4 tsp. pepper
1/8 tsp. salt

1. Combine to make marinade:
1/4 cup white wine vinegar
2 tablespoons green onions - minced
2 tablespoons lime juice
2 teaspoons olive oil
1 tablespoon dijon mustard
1/4 teaspoon pepper
1/8 teaspoon salt

2. Place in marinade, cover and refrigerate for 1 hour:
1 pound yellow fin tuna - cut in 1" cubes

3. While fish is marinating, prepare:
1 spaghetti squash

Cut in half lengthwise discarding seeds. Place cut side down in a Dutch oven. Add water to make a 2 inch depth. Bring to boil and simmer 20 minutes or until tender. Drain water. Using a fork, remove strands from squash and then discard shells.

Or, the squash may be cooked in microwave.

Fresh Tuna Kabobs Continued

4. Spread squash on serving plate and sprinkle with:
2 tablespoons fresh parsley - chopped
2 teaspoons butter
Keep squash warm.

5. Remove fish from marinade reserving marinade for use later.

6. Alternate fish on kabob skewers with the following vegetables:
8 large mushroom caps
1 cup zucchini - sliced 1/2 inch thick
1/2 cup sweet red pepper - seeded and sliced
1/2 cup onion - cut in 1 inch pieces

7. Grill uncovered 6 minutes on each side until fish flakes easily. Baste with remaining marinade during grilling. Serve over squash.

4 Servings
per serving:
3 protein blocks
3-1/2 carbohydrate blocks
3 fat blocks

Count Nutrients Not Calories

The question is not, "How little should I eat?" but "How well can I eat?" When you ask the wrong questions, you'll never get the answers you're seeking. The natural vitality, nutritional quality and balance of the food you put into your mouth is much more important than the number of calories it contains. So put away your fat finder and calorie counter and follow these simple plans. We hope to help you take your focus off "dieting" and "weight" so you will be free to adopt a healthy, energetic lifestyle based on your individual needs. This is a process, not an end point. As this process evolves you will not only become thinner, but healthier: physically, mentally and emotionally.

21 Healing Dinners

almond butter

#1— 4 blocks: **BAKED FISH SUPREME**
(page 62)
1/4 cup onion
1/2 cup red pepper
1 cup yellow squash
1/2 cup brown rice sauteed in
1 tsp. olive oil

#2— 4 blocks: **LEMON BAKED TURKEY
BREAST** *(page 82)*
1 cup green beans
2/3 baked sweet potato
Cabbage slaw (1-1/2 cup shredded
cabbage mixed with 1-1/2 tbsp.
mayonnaise with 3 grams
fat/tbsp.)

#3— 4 blocks: **ITALIAN STYLE TURKEY
STEAKS** *(page 63)*
ZUCCHINI MEDLEY *(page 64)*
1/2 cup wild rice
2 pecans, chopped

#4— 4 blocks: **CHILI** *(page 65)*
2 Wasa Crackers spread with
1-1/2 tsp. almond butter

#5— 3 blocks: **CONFETTI TURKEY LOAF**
(page 66) 1 serving
1/2 cup cooked kamut tossed with
2/3 tsp. butter and
Italian herbs to taste

#6— 4 blocks: **CHICKEN & ZUCCHINI BAKE**

(page 67) 1 serving
3/4 C cooked amaranth pasta
tossed with 2/3 tsp olive oil
and herbs

#7— 3 blocks: **SPICY BAKED OATS** *(page 68)*
3 **TURKEY NUGGETS** *(page 30)*
3 pecan halves, chopped, sprinkled
on oats when served

#8— 4 blocks: **CHICKEN STIR FRY** *(page 69)*
1/2 cup cooked brown rice
3 raw almonds, slivered

#9— 4 blocks: **CHICKEN VEGETABLE SOUP**
(page 71)
1 Wasa cracker with
1 tsp. almond butter

#10— 3 blocks: **MINNESOTA TURKEY &
WILD RICE CASSEROLE**
(page 72)
1/2 tsp. butter melted on top

#11— 4 blocks: **SQUASH WITH SPAGHETTI**
(page 73) one serving
3 oz. broiled chicken breast topped
with 1/2 cup pasta sauce
2 cups organic salad greens
tossed with 2 tbsp. **HEALTHY
SALAD DRESSING** *(page 44)*

#12— 4 blocks: 1/4 lb. organic beef patty
TOSSED SPINACH SALAD
(page 75)
1 oz. shredded cheese
1 tbsp. **HEALTHY SALAD
DRESSING** *(page 44)*

2/3 cup hash browns

#13— 3 blocks: 1 serving **BAKED TOFU**
(*page 77*) sprinkled on
2 cups fresh greens tossed with
1 cup diced raw vegetables,
1 tbsp. **HEALTHY SALAD
DRESSING** (*page 44*)
1/2 cup cubed pineapple

#14— 3 blocks: **CAJUN BEANS**
(*page 78*) 1 serving
1 oz. shredded cheese
TOFU GUACAMOLE
(*page 27*) 1 serving

#15— 3 blocks: 1 serving **CAJUN FISH
FILLETS** (*page 79*)
2 cups steamed vegetables
3 thin slices avocado
1 cup strawberries

#16— 4 blocks: **LEMON VEGETABLE FISH
SUPREME**
(*page 80*) 1/3 recipe
1 cup salad greens topped with
lemon
1 small baked potato,
1 tbsp. sour cream

#17— 4 blocks: **SPAGHETTI PIE**
(*page 41*) 1 serving

1 tbsp. grated Parmesan cheese
4 cups salad greens
1 tsp. olive oil mixed with vinegar
and herbs for dressing

#18— 4 blocks: **STEAMED FISH AND
VEGETABLES** (*page 81*)
1 serving
Salad with 1 cup raw spinach
1 slice onion separated into rings
1/2 orange, sectioned
1 tsp. grated Parmesan cheese
tossed with olive oil and vinegar
dressing

#19— 4 blocks: 1 Boca Burger topped with 1 oz. of
sliced cheese
2 cups mixed greens tossed with
1/3 tsp olive oil with vinegar and
herbs
1 serving **TOFU PUMPKIN PIE**
(*page 28*)

#20— 3 blocks: 4 soy sausage links
1 serving **TOFU CHEESECAKE**
(*page 55*) topped with
BLUEBERRY FRUIT GLAZE
(*page 32*) 1 serving

#21— 4 blocks: **SWORDFISH WITH POTA-
TOES** (*page 82*) 1 serving
TOSSED SPINACH SALAD
(*page 76*) 1 serving
HEALTHY SALAD DRESSING
(*page 44*) 1 tbsp.

Baked Fish Supreme

Ingredients:

1 1/4 lbs. (20 oz.) Sole, Orange Ruffie or any white fish
1/2 cup lemon juice (or 1/4 cup each of vinegar and water)
1 tsp. parsley
1 tbsp. celery

4 Servings

per serving:
3 protein blocks
0 carbohydrate blocks
0 fat blocks

Preheat oven to 350. Prepare oil sprayed baking dish.

1. Cut into 1" cubes
1 1/4 pound fish

2. Combine and pour over fish:
1/2 cup lemon juice (or 1/4 cup each of vinegar and water)
1 teaspoon parsley - diced
1 tablespoon celery - minced

3. Crush and sprinkle over fish:
2 Lite Rye Wasa Crackers

4. Bake for 20 minutes or until fish is flaky.

❋ **To Complete the Meal—** *serve with 1/2 cup brown rice, 12 asparagus spears and 1 teaspoon butter.*

Italian Style Turkey Steaks

Ingredients:

2 tsp. olive oil
1 pound turkey breast
1 cup mushrooms - sliced
1/4 cup chicken broth
(fat free)
2 cups fresh tomatoes
1/2 tsp. onion flakes
1/4 tsp. oregano leaves

4 Servings

per serving:
4 protein blocks
1/2 carbohydrate block
1/2 fat block

1. Brown the following in a skillet - remove after browned:

2 teaspoon olive oil
1 pound turkey breast - sliced into 1/4" slices
1 cup mushrooms - sliced

2. Add to skillet:

1/4 cup chicken broth
2 cups fresh tomatoes - chopped
1/2 teaspoon onion flakes - dried
1/4 teaspoon oregano leaves - dried
salt and pepper to taste

3. Add to skillet:

Turkey breast and mushrooms

4. Bring mixture to boil:

Reduce heat, cover and cook until turkey is tender (approximately 10 minutes).

❋ ***To Complete the Meal—***
serve with 1/2 baked potato with 2 tablespoons sour cream and 2 cups mixed steamed vegetables.

Zucchini Medley

Ingredients:

1 cup zucchini
1/2 cup green pepper
1/4 tsp. black pepper
1/4 tsp. dried oregano leaves
1 cup summer yellow squash
1 tsp. olive
1/2 cup onion
1 clove garlic

---

1 Serving

per serving:
0 protein blocks
2 carbohydrate blocks
3 fat blocks

---

1. Heat in skillet and saute for 5 minutes:

1 teaspoon olive oil
1/2 cup onion - chopped
1 clove garlic - minced

2. Add and cook until tender:

1 cup zucchini - thinly sliced
1/2 cup green pepper - chopped

1/4 teaspoon black pepper
1/4 teaspoon dried oregano leaves
1 cup summer yellow squash - thinly sliced

❋ ***To Complete the Meal—***
Serve with 3 ounce organic beef patty on 1/2 slice rye bread.

Chili

Ingredients:

1-1/2 oz. of sun-dried tomatoes
1 cup boiling water
2 pounds turkey
1 cup onion
1 cup green pepper
2 cloves garlic
2 tbsp. chili powder
1 tsp. cumin
1 tsp. oregano leaves
1/4 tsp. Tabasco sauce
6 medium fresh tomatoes
1 can of organic tomato soup
16 oz. can of kidney beans
10 large black olives

6 Servings

per 2 cup serving:
4 protein blocks
3 carbohydrate blocks
1 fat blocks

1. In food processor, puree and set aside:
1-1/2 ounces sun-dried tomatoes
1 cup boiling water

2. Brown the in 2 quart sauce pan:
2 pounds of fresh ground turkey

3. Add and cook until tender:
1 cup onion - chopped
1 cup green pepper - chopped
2 cloves of garlic - minced (to taste)

4. Add tomato mixture plus the following to sauce pan.

5. Heat to boiling, cover and simmer for 1 hour - stirring occasionally.

2 tablespoons chili powder
1 teaspoon cumin
1 teaspoon oregano leaves - dried
1/4 teaspoon Tabasco sauce
6 medium fresh tomatoes - diced
1 can organic tomato soup

6. Add and heat to boiling.
16 ounces of kidney beans - canned

7. Simmer until desired consistency (approximately 20 minutes).

8. Top with:
10 large sliced black olives

❋ To Complete the Meal—
Serve with 2 cups romaine leaves, 1 cup fresh salad vegetables and 2/3 tsp olive oil.

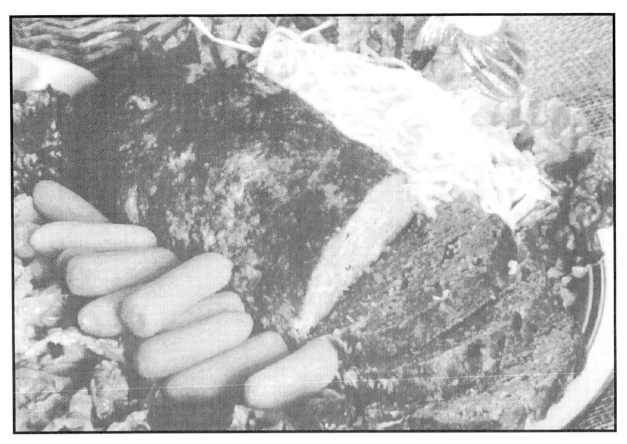

Confetti Turkey Loaf

Ingredients:

2 tsp. extra virgin olive oil
1 medium onion
1/2 cup frozen mixed bell pepper (red, green, yellow)
1 1/4 lbs. extra lean ground turkey
2 organic egg whites
1 medium carrot
1/2 tsp. salt
1/4 tsp. pepper
1 tablespoon fennel seed or dill weed (optional)
1/2 cup oats, thick rolled or steel cut)
1/2 cup soy milk

6 Servings

per serving:

3 protein blocks
1 carbohydrate blocks
1 fat block

Preheat oven to 350°.

1. Coat a 9X12 inch baking pan with cooking spray.

2. Heat in a medium skillet and saute´until soft:

1 2/3 teaspoon olive oil
1/2 cup onion - chopped
1/2 cup mixed bell pepper - chopped

3. Transfer onion and pepper to a medium bowl and let cool slightly (5 minutes).

4. In a two cup measuring cup, combine and soak 5 minutes:

1/2 cup oats
1/2 cup soy milk

5. To the saute´ed vegetables add:

1 1/4 pound lean ground turkey
2 egg whites
1 medium carrot - shredded
1/2 teaspoon salt
1/4 teaspoon pepper
1 tablespoon fennel seed (optional)
1/2 cup oats
1/2 cup soymilk

6. Mix all ingredients together with hands until well blended. Shape the meat into a loaf in the prepared pan. Bake one hour.

※ ***To Complete the Meal—*** *serve with 1 cup steamed vegetables and 1 cup hot spaghetti squash tossed with 2/3 teaspoon butter and fresh Italian herbs.*

Chicken and Zucchini Bake

Ingredients:

1 pound boneless chicken
1 clove garlic
15 oz. organic tomato sauce
2 tsp. extra virgin olive oil
2 cups zucchini
1 tbsp. fresh thyme
1 tbsp. lemon peel
1 tbsp. fresh basil leaves
1 tbsp. fresh oregano leaves

4 Servings

per serving:
4 protein blocks
1 carbohydrate block
1-1/2 fat blocks

Preheat oven to 375°.

1. In large skillet, sauté:
2 teaspoons olive oil
1 clove garlic - minced

2. Add chicken, cover, reduce heat and cook for 30 minutes

3. Pour into oil sprayed baking dish:
15 ounces tomato sauce

4. Place the following in a 9x13" baking dish:
2 cups zucchini - julienne
1 tablespoon fresh basil leaves
1 tablespoon fresh oregano leaves
1 tablespoon fresh thyme
cooked chicken mixture

5. Sprinkle over the top:
1 tablespoon lemon peel - grated

6. Cover with foil and bake for 30 minutes.

❋ ***To Complete the Meal—*** *serve over 1/2 cup cooked spelt and top with 1 1/2 tea-spoons raw pine nuts.*

Spicy Baked Oats

Ingredients:

1 cup steal cut oats
1 tbsp. extra virgin olive oil
1/2 cup onion
2 cups water (or vegetable broth)
2 tbsp. fresh thyme
3 tbsp. fresh sage
1/4 cup celery
1/4 cup squash
1 tsp. salt

---

4 Servings

per serving:
0 protein blocks
3 carbohydrate blocks
2 fat blocks

---

1. In large skillet, sauté until tender:

1 tablespoon olive oil
1/2 cup onion - chopped

2. Add and sauté an additional 5 minutes:

1/4 cup celery - diced
1/4 cup squash (butternut, acorn, zucchini) - cubed
3 tablespoons sage (fresh or dried)
2 tablespoons fresh thyme
1 cup steal cut oats

3. Transfer to oil-sprayed baking dish. Add the following:

1 teaspoon salt
2 cups water (or broth)

4. Bake 350 for 30 minutes or until liquid is absorbed.

❋ *To Complete the Meal— serve with 3 ounces turkey breast topped with 3 chopped almonds.*

Lemon Baked Turkey Breast

Ingredients:

*3 pounds turkey breast or
turkey tenderloin
1/2 cup chicken broth
1 clove garlic
1 whole lemon
1 cup yellow onion
dried basil and sage
salt*

---

12 Servings

per serving:
4 protein blocks
0 carbohydrate blocks
0 fat blocks

**1. Preheat oven to 325.
Place in baking dish:**
3 pounds of chicken or turkey

2. Pour over the meat:
1/2 cup chicken broth

**3. Cut slits in top of breast
Insert:**
*1 clove of garlic - thinly
sliced*

4. Arrange on top of turkey:
1 whole lemon - thinly sliced

5. Place around the turkey:
1 cup yellow onion - sliced

6. Sprinkle over the turkey:
*dried basil and sage (approx-
imately. 1/4 to 1/2 teaspoon
of each)
salt to taste*

**7. Bake uncovered until
meat begins to brown then
cover with foil. Bake for 1
hour or until meat is fork
tender. Let meat stand for a
few minutes before slicing.
Garnish with parsley and
serve.**

✳ ***To Complete the Meal—***
*serve with Spicy Baked Oats
(page 68) tossed with 1/3 teaspoon butter or olive oil.*

Chicken Stir Fry (With Tomato and Green Peppers)

Ingredients:

1 pound skinless chicken breast
3 large fresh tomatoes
1 green pepper
1 medium onion
2 tbsp. Bragg Liquid aminos
1 tbsp. white wine
salt
2 tbsp. vegetable glycerine
1-1/2 tbsp. corn starch
1/2 cup water

1. Cut into 1" cubes (slice across grain to enhance tenderness):

1 pound chicken breast

2. Combine in small bowl and add the chicken cubes to:

2 tablespoons Bragg Liquid Aminos
1 tablespoon white wine
salt to taste

3. Prepare the following for stir frying:

large fresh tomatoes - cut in wedges
1 green pepper - cut in large chunks
1 medium onion - thinly sliced
1 clove garlic - minced

4. Have ready:

2 tablespoons vegetable glycerine

Chicken Stir Fry Continued

5. Combine the following in small bowl:
1-1/2 tablespoons corn starch
1/2 cup water

6. Heat in wok and stir fry marinated chicken cubes for 3 minutes:
1 tablespoon olive oil

7. Move chicken up side of wok and add the prepared vegetables and vegetable glycerine cooking 3-5 minutes until vegetables are cooked (do not overcook): (Make sure 1 cup of liquid is retained in bottom of wok at all times. May be necessary to add additional liquid.)

8. Add cornstarch mixture to liquid in wok stirring until thickened.

✳ ***To Complete the Meal—*** *serve over 3/4 cup cooked brown rice with 6 raw almonds, sliced.*

4 Servings
per serving:
4 protein blocks
1 carbohydrate block
2-1/2 fat blocks

Chicken Vegetable Soup

Ingredients:
1 pound chicken
1 cup onion
2 tbsp. olive oil
5 cans chicken broth, nonfat, preservative free
1/2 cup barley (uncooked)
2 cups fresh tomato
1/2 tsp. salt
1 tsp. garlic powder
1 tsp. basil leaves
1/2 tsp. thyme
1 tsp. tomato powder (optional)
1/4 tsp. red pepper flakes
1-1/2 cups frozen mixed vegetables or fresh vegetable of choice

1. Heat in skillet:
2 tablespoons olive oil

2. Brown the following ingredients in 4 quart sauce pan:
1 pound raw ground or diced chicken
1 cup onion - diced

2. Add:
5 cans chicken broth
1/2 cup barley (uncooked)

3. Stir in the remaining ingredients and adjust seasonings to taste:
2 cups fresh tomato - diced
1/2 teaspoon salt
1/2 teaspoon thyme - dried
1 teaspoon garlic powder
1 teaspoon basil leaves - dried
1 teaspoon tomato powder
1/4 teaspoon red pepper flakes

4. Bring mixture to a boil. Reduce heat and simmer for 1/2 hour or until barley is tender.

5. Add and heat to serving temperature:
1-1/2 cups fresh or frozen mixed vegetables.

✳ ***To Complete the Meal—*** *serve with 4 Wasa crackers and 1 teaspoon pine nuts.*

---

6 Servings
per 2 cup serving:
4 protein blocks
2-1/2 carbohydrate blocks
3 fat blocks

Minnesota Turkey and Wild Rice Casserole

Ingredients:

1-1/4 pounds turkey breast
1 cup celery
1 cup green pepper
1 cup onion
2 tsp. olive oil
9 black olives
8 oz. canned water chestnuts
1 cup wild rice
2 tbsp. Bragg Liquid Aminos
2 cups chicken broth (fat free)
2 tbsp. flour
1 tsp. garlic powder
1 tsp. poultry seasoning
24 almonds

6 Servings

per serving:
3 protein blocks
3 carbohydrate blocks
3 fat blocks

Preheat oven to 350°.

1. Rinse wild rice and soak for 2 hours in 2 cups of boiling water.

2. Brown in skillet:
2 teaspoons olive oil
1 cup onion - chopped
1 cup green pepper - chopped
1 cup celery - thinly sliced
1-1/2 pounds turkey breast

3. Add to skillet:
9 black olives - sliced
8 ounces canned water chestnuts - drained, sliced
1 cup prepared wild rice
2 tablespoons Bragg Liquid Aminos
2 cups chicken broth

4. Add and stir until well blended:
2 tablespoons flour
1 teaspoon garlic powder
1 teaspoon poultry seasoning

5. Bake in an oil-sprayed, covered 3-quart casserole 45 minutes until liquid is absorbed.

6. Garnish each serving with 4 chopped almonds and serve.

Chicken with Spaghetti Squash & Pasta

Ingredients:

6 boneless, skinless chicken breasts (3 oz. each)
1 medium spaghetti squash (3 lbs.)
8 oz. spaghetti
1/2 cup fresh parsley
1/2 cup onion
2 cloves garlic
2 tbsp. extra virgin olive oil
4 tbsp. fresh oregano
4 tbsp. fresh grated Parmesan cheese
pasta sauce (preservative free)

1. Prepare as follows:
1 medium spaghetti squash

Cut in half lengthwise. Discard seeds. Place cut side down in Dutch oven. Add water to 2" depth. Bring to boil, reduce heat and simmer 20 minutes, or until tender. Drain water and cool. Using a fork, remove squash from shell in long strands and place in large bowl.

2. Cook as directed on package, drain in colander and rinse with hot water:
8 ounces spaghetti, broken in half before cooking.

3. While squash and pasta are cooking, sauté in medium skillet until golden:
2 teaspoons olive oil
1/2 cup onion - diced
2 cloves garlic - finely diced

4. Heat broiler and broil 4 to 5 minutes on each side:
6- 3 oz. chicken breasts

5. In a small saucepan, warm:
1/3 jar pasta sauce (preservative free)

Chicken with Spaghetti Squash & Pasta continued

6. Toss together in a bowl:
Cooked squash and spaghetti
Onion and garlic sauteed in
olive oil
4 tablespoons fresh grated
Parmesan cheese
4 tablespoons fresh oregano -
chopped

7. To serve, place one chicken breast on each plate. Drizzle 2 tablespoons of **heated spaghetti sauce over each breast and serve with one cup of spaghetti squash and spaghetti mixture.**

❋ *To Complete the Meal—serve with 4 cups of mixed greens tossed with 2 teaspoons Healthy Salad Dressing (page 44) per serving.*

6 Servings
per serving (one chicken breast with one cup pasta & squash)
4 protein blocks
3 carbohydrate blocks
3 fat blocks

Tossed Spinach Salad

Ingredients:
*4 cups spinach leaves - well
cleaned and dried
1 cup onion - sliced
1 cup mushrooms - sliced
1 cup fresh tomato - diced*

**1. Toss all ingredients
together.**

❋ ***To Complete the Meal—***
*top with 3 oz grilled chicken
breast, 2/3 cup fresh
raspberries, 2 teaspoons
Healthy Salad Dressing
(page 44), and serve with
2 Wasa crackers.*

4 Servings
per serving:
0 protein blocks
1 carbohydrate blocks
0 fat blocks

Baked Tofu

Ingredients:

1 pound conventional tofu (freeze overnight, and thaw prior to using).
1/4 cup Bragg Liquid Aminos
2 tbsp. water
1 tbsp. peanut butter
1/4 tsp. black pepper

2 Servings
per serving:
2-1/2 protein blocks
0 carbohydrate blocks
1/2 fat blocks

Freeze overnight:
1 pound conventional tofu

1. Thaw frozen tofu and drain water from block by placing in dish towel and squeezing out liquid. Crumble tofu and mix in a bowl with:
1/4 cup Bragg Liquid Aminos
2 tablespoons water
1 tablespoon peanut butter
1/4 teaspoon black pepper

2. Mix with hands until liquid mixture is evenly absorbed into tofu.

3. Bake in 8" pan at 450 for 30 minutes stirring every 10 minutes (to prevent sticking and for even browning).

❋ ***To Complete the Meal—*** *sauté 3/4 cup green pepper, 1/2 cup onions, 2/3 cup hash brown potatoes, one egg white and Baked Tofu in 2/3 teaspoon olive oil.*

Cajun Beans

Ingredients:

2 tsp. olive oil
*8 oz. cooked chicken breast
(or cooked turkey)*
1 cup celery
1/4 cup onion
1/2 cup green pepper
15 oz. kidney beans
15 oz. pinto beans
15 oz. black beans
1 bay leaf
1 cup water
1 clove garlic
1 tsp. Cajun spices

**1. Brown the following in
2 quart saucepan:**

2 teaspoon olive oil
1 cup celery - diced
1/4 cup onion - chopped
*1/2 cup green pepper -
chopped*

2. Add to saucepan:

15 ounces kidney beans
15 ounces pinto beans
15 ounces black beans
*8 ounces cooked chicken
breast (or cooked turkey)*
1 cup water

1 clove garlic - minced
1 bay leaf
*1 teaspoon Cajun spices - to
taste*

**3. Bring to a boil, and then
simmer at low heat for 20
minutes.**

❊ *To Complete the Meal—
serve with 1/8 cup Tofu
Guacamole Dressing (page
27) and sprinkle with 1 ounce
shredded cheese.*

6 Servings
per serving:
3 protein blocks
4 carbohydrate blocks
1 fat blocks

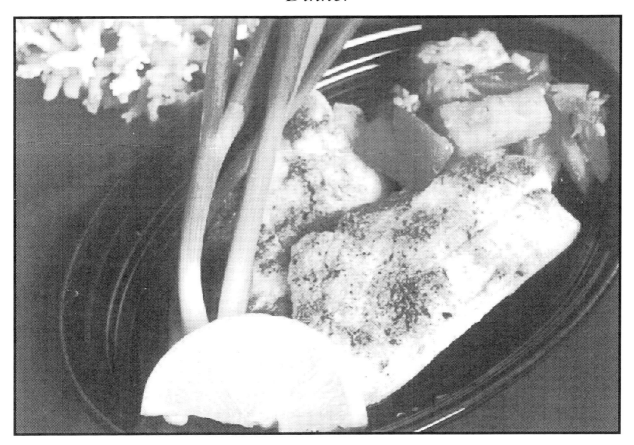

Cajun Fish Fillets

Ingredients:

1 1/4 lbs. Sole, Orange Ruffie or any white fish
1/4 cup fresh lemon juice & pulp
2 tsp. paprika
1 tsp. sea salt
1 tsp. garlic powder
1 tsp. onion powder
1/4 tsp. black pepper
1/4 tsp. white pepper
1/4 tsp. dried oregano leaves
1/4 tsp. dried thyme

1. Place in nonstick baking pan:
1 1/4 pound fish

2. Sprinkle over fillets:
1/4 cup fresh lemon juice & pulp

3. Combine in small bowl to create "Cajun" seasoning:
2 teaspoons paprika
1 teaspoon sea salt
1 teaspoon garlic powder
1 teaspoon onion powder
1/4 teaspoon black pepper
1/4 teaspoon white pepper

1/4 teaspoon dried oregano leaves
1/4 teaspoon dried thyme

4. Sprinkle "Cajun" seasoning to taste on fish.

5. Bake uncovered 350°, for 20 minutes.

❋ ***To Complete the Meal—*** *serve with 1/3 cup sliced sweet potatoes, 1/3 cup white potatoes and 1 cup broccoli, steamed, topped with 1 teaspoon butter.*

4 Servings
per serving:
3 protein blocks
0 carbohydrate blocks
0 fat blocks

Lemon Vegetable Fish Supreme

Ingredients:
1 1/4 pound Sole, Orange Ruffie or any white fish
1/2 cup lemon juice
1 tbsp. lemon peel
2 cups zucchini
1/8 tsp. salt
1/8 tsp. tarragon
dried thyme, basil and pepper

---

4 Servings

per serving:
3 protein blocks
1/2 carbohydrate blocks
0 fat blocks

---

1. In oil sprayed baking dish, place the following:
1 1/4 pound fish
1/2 cup lemon juice

2. Cover with foil. Bake at 375° for 25 minutes. Remove from oven.

3. While baking, combine the following to spoon over baked fish:
1 tablespoon lemon peel - grated
2 cups zucchini - shredded
1/8 teaspoon salt
1/8 teaspoon tarragon - dried
dash of each dried thyme, basil and pepper

4. Cover with foil and return to oven to bake an additional 8-10 minutes. (Fish is cooked when it flakes easily with fork). Garnish with lemon cartwheel twists.

✳ *To Complete the Meal— serve with 1/2 cup cooked wild rice, 2 cups mixed greens and 2 tablespoons Healthy Salad Dressing (page 44).*

Steamed Fish and Vegetables

Ingredients:

4 cups potatoes
2 cups zucchini
2 cups carrots
2 cups green beans
2 cups peppers,
2 cups broccoli,
2 cups cauliflower,
2 cups onions
1 3/4 lb. fish fillets
basil or dill weed

1. In a sauce pan, bring to a boil, 1 inch of water. Place steamer basket on top of pan and cook for 10 minutes:

4 cups potatoes (white or sweet - scrubbed and sliced)

2. Add the following to steamer basket and steam an additional 10 minutes:

(All remaining cleaned and diced vegetables)
12 ounces of fish fillet
basil or dill - to taste

※ *To Complete the Meal—use 1 teaspoon olive oil or butter on each serving of vegetables.*

6 Servings

per serving:
3 protein blocks
3 carbohydrate blocks
0 fat blocks

Swordfish with Potatoes

Ingredients:

4 - 6 oz. swordfish steaks
1 pound potatoes - frozen hash browns, plain
1/2 cup pasta sauce
2-1/2 cups fresh tomatoes
1 tbsp. lemon juice
4 tbsp. fresh parsley
1 tbsp. fresh basil leaves
1 tbsp. fresh oregano leaves
1/2 tbsp. fresh thyme
1/2 cup onion
2 cloves
1/4 cup vegetable broth

4 Servings

per serving:
4 protein blocks
3 carbohydrate blocks
0 fat blocks

Preheat oven to 375°.

1. In ovenproof skillet, sauté until tender:
1/2 cup onion - chopped
2 cloves garlic - minced
1/4 cup vegetable broth

2. Add and bring to a boil:
1/2 cup pasta sauce
2-1/2 cups fresh tomatoes - diced
1 tablespoon lemon juice
4 tablespoons fresh parsley
1 tablespoon fresh oregano leaves
1 tablespoon fresh basil leaves
1/2 tablespoon fresh thyme - ground

3. Reduce heat and add:
4 swordfish steaks
(6 oz. each)

4. Center the fish steaks on top of sauce. Place the following on top of fish:
1 pound potatoes - frozen

5. Spoon a portion of the sauce over fish and potatoes. Cover and bake 30 minutes until fish flakes and potatoes are tender.

✳ *To Complete the Meal—Serve with Tossed Spinach Salad (page 75) and Healthy Salad Dressing (page 44).*

Stocking Your Picture Book Kitchen

SHOPPING TIPS

The first step to cooking Zone healthy is knowing how to shop and what foods to stock up on. The following shopping tips will make building Zone meals a breeze. Remember the goal is to prepare nutritious Zone meals quickly and easily without continuously reinventing the wheel at each meal.

To prepare meals quickly, it helps to buy ingredients in their most usable form. It may mean that you purchase chicken or turkey skinned and boned or precooked deli meats from a natural foods store or local co-op. Cheese could be pre-sliced or shredded. Salad greens could be prewashed, sliced, and in bags. Fresh fruit may also be cubed and packaged. Stock up on favorite fruits and vegetables, both fresh and frozen.

PROTEIN CHOICES

From the Meat Counter

Lean red meat– is not fattening, but the fat it contains (arachidonic acid) is not the best choice for staying in "the Zone", especially if you suffer from chronic pain. If you love red meat, treat yourself once or twice a week. If you can find organic meat, include it as often as your budget allows. Organic meat and poultry is free of antibiotics, growth hormones and toxic chemicals that interfere with healing. Choose leg and loin cuts most often and remove visible fat. For ease and convenience, choose serving size cuts like steaks, chops, fillets, tenderloins, and shish kabobs or 95%, or better, lean ground meats.

Plenty of poultry– white or breast meat with the skin removed is best. Breast cuts of chicken and turkey are very low in fat. Substitute ground chicken or turkey breast for ground beef in chili and casseroles. Be sure to purchase ground breast without added fat or skin. Ground turkey often contains more fat than regular ground beef. Again, we encourage you to purchase organic or free-range poultry when possible. You will be amazed at the difference in taste between a roasted, organic or free-range chicken and one from the meat counter of your usual grocery store. Baby boomers comment that organic chicken reminds them of the chicken from years ago when our food supply was less polluted.

For convenience and emergencies, have cans of chicken or turkey in the cupboard or in your desk drawer at work. They are great for snacks. Swanson's is a brand easily found on grocery shelves. At the health food store, look for frozen organic chicken or turkey sausage or hot dogs without nitrates or other chemical additives. They are a healthy way to add protein at breakfast.

Fish– Low in fat or not, fresh, frozen or canned in water, fish is an excellent protein choice. Fish contains omega-3 fatty acids--the healthy fats. All fish cooks quickly and water-packed tuna, canned salmon, sardines and trout come ready to eat in a "pop top can" for convenient snacking.

Eggs– certainly don't deserve the reputation they have acquired during the past decade of cholesterol bashing and fat-free merchandising. Eggs are one of the most readily available sources of protein we can consume. They have long been regarded as the standard against which all other protein is judged. One egg provides one protein block. Like red meat, the yolks contain arachidonic acid which can take you out of the Zone. However, some arachidonic acid is necessary for balance and very important for brain health.

Cholesterol is also necessary for hormone function. Cholesterol only needs to be avoided if it has been oxidized. This oxidized cholesterol is found in foods that have been processed: powdered milk, powdered eggs, processed baked goods (muffins, cakes, donuts, etc.), and cheese and meats, such as sausage, that have been aged.

Yolks from grocery store eggs retain toxic residues from the growth hormones, pesticides and antibiotics fed to most commercially grown chickens, and we recommend you avoid them for this reason. However, if you are fortunate enough to find free-range eggs from a local farmer or organic eggs at your co-op, eating the whole egg is healthy. Because of what these chickens are fed, the yolks of their eggs have less saturated fat and more of the essential omega-3 and omega-6 fatty acids necessary for hormone balance. Again, you will be surprised at the dramatic flavor differences between organic eggs and those commercially available at your supermarket. They bring back those memories from childhood again--especially if you were raised on a farm!

Other animal proteins– Today there are many meats available at your supermarket that may be new to you. Experiment for variety. Buffalo, ostrich, rabbit and venison come to mind. You may know of meats in your part of the country or have lean, wild game in the freezer if you have a hunter in the family.

From the Dairy Case

Non-fat dairy products--provide essential protein, calcium and vitamins without saturated animal fat. Best choices are skim milk, nonfat yogurt and dry curd cottage cheese.

Plain, non-fat yogurt– makes a healthy substitute for sour cream and creamy dressings for dipping vegetables or topping salads and potatoes. Fat free sour cream is not a healthy choice for healing as it contains many additives and refined carbohydrates.

While on the subject of additives and carbohydrates, lets examine yogurt carefully, too. A half cup of plain, non-fat yogurt has an easy to remember balance and makes an ideal snack with the addition of three raw almonds. It is equal to one protein building block, one carbohydrate building block and one fat building block. A half cup of vanilla flavored yogurt provides only 1/2 block of protein and two blocks of carbohydrate– a one to four ratio. The ratios of fruit flavored yogurts can be more off-balance– even the sugar free varieties!

You may discover, as we did, that you can eat more naturally and control balance easier by adding your own flavors: high protein vanilla fla-

vored powders, or natural protein powder plus vanilla and fruits of your choice.

The most healing yogurts are the organic, natural ones with active cultures that you find at the co-op or whole foods grocery. Choose plain, sugar-free yogurt without artificial sweetener.

Cottage Cheese– next on the list of quality dairy products. Most cottage cheese in your grocer's dairy case is loaded with chemicals and carbohydrates. Old Home dry curd cottage cheese, available to us in the Midwest, is the best we have found. It's only ingredient is cultured skim milk and 1/4 cup provides more than a block of protein and only one gram of carbohydrate. Friendship low-fat cottage cheese from Friendship, New York, can be found in whole food stores and co-ops. It's only ingredient is cultured skim milk and 1/4 cup yields over a block of protein and only 2 grams of carbohydrate.

A cottage cheese distributed by Kraft foods and easily found at major retail grocery chains, is Breakstone's, 2% fat. It gives you one block of protein and only 2 grams of carbohydrate per 1/4 cup. However, it contains more additives--modified food starch, salt, guar gum and natural flavor. Though many brands of non-fat cottage cheese provide the same ratio of protein to carbohydrate as as the ones we recommend, the ingredient list on most non-fat cottage cheese is very long and includes preservatives, thickeners and artificial colors. So it pays to become a food detective when shopping for ingredients to prepare our *Picture Book for Zone Cook* recipes. Many brands of fat-free cottage cheese contain as much carbohydrate as protein.

Cheese– comes next. Avoid the fat-free cheeses. They are loaded with sodium, sugar and artificial flavor enhancers! They seldom taste as good as the real thing and often leave you craving more! Use real cheese, but sparingly, to add flavor to a meal, because most good cheeses are high in fat and cholesterol.

If you don't eat meat, you may rely more heavily on cheese for a protein source. If so, the part-skim varieties are a healthier choice as they have a protein and fat content similar to lean meat. There are so many wonderful cheeses available today, and many of them are made from the milk of animals other than cows (goats for example), that we can't begin to list them all. A good low-fat choice is part skim mozzarella, with less than five grams of fat per ounce. Other healthy choices include farmer's cheese (available in blocks and in curd form), real Parmesan, freshly grated (adds a dash of flavor to any dish), ricotta, Swiss and Jarlsberg.

It's healthiest to limit your use of hard cheese to an occasional ounce here and there. An ounce of shredded hard cheese goes a long way in adding flavor to eggs, a salad or chili.

Vegetarian Proteins

Tofu– that white stuff that looks like cream cheese, but jiggles like jello! Made from soybean curds, tofu is an excellent source of protein. Three ounces provide one block of protein. Tofu is highly digestible, inexpensive, low in saturated fats, low in chemical toxins and contains essential fatty acids. Mori-Nu is a brand that is easy to find. It comes in soft, firm and extra firm varieties. It's easy to use and easy to store. People sensitive to soy can usually tolerate this brand. Another brand that is easy to find is White Wave. White Wave is organic and also easily tolerated by those with soy sensitivities. Your local co-op grocery may stock organic tofu, bulk in the cooler. Ask to see what is available at your market.

Soy milk– WestSoy Natural Organic is king of the soy milks for providing protein. One cup provides one block of protein and only 4 grams of carbohydrate. Next comes Original EdenSoy organic soy beverage. It yields one block of protein and one block of carbohydrate in 3/4 of a cup. All other brands and even different varieties of these two brands contain two to four times more carbohydrate than protein. Be especially careful of vanilla, carob and fat-free varieties. Like yogurt, they are loaded with rice syrup, corn syrup and other refined carbohydrates.

You will find yourself becoming a carbohydrate detective, just like us-- looking for the hidden carbohydrates in packaged foods. What a shift! Dietitians have been busy programming us to look for hidden fat the last ten years while the food giants have been busy adding refined sugars to their fat-free packaged food to make them edible! At least young mothers are becoming more aware and boycotting the major baby food producers who add sugar to their products. Carbohydrate addiction can begin at an early age!

Soy products– that resemble meat are everywhere. Look for soy burgers (Boca burgers are a favorite of ours), soy hot dogs and sausage made from textured vegetable protein. You can also find soy cheese, soy yogurt and even soy ice cream! However, just because a product is made from soy and found in a health food store, you can't assume it's a healing food. It's important to always read labels. Many soy products contain refined sugars and preservatives, such as citric acid, which interfere with healing.

Beans– Though considered a protein source for vegetarians, beans contain twice as much carbohydrate as they do protein, and the protein they do contain is not very available to your body. Consider beans and legumes as carbohydrates when balancing Zone meals.

A fun addition to your diet, sweet green soybeans, are now available frozen in many large grocery stores. They contain a more favorable protein to carbohydrate balance.

CARBOHYDRATE CHOICES

Fruits and Vegetables

Build your carbohydrate blocks around fruits and vegetables and you'll come out a winner. Most of the nutrients your body needs come from the produce section, not the bread section. Fruits and vegetables make convenient carbohydrates to combine with meat, cheese or tofu and nuts for one block snacks. Choose seasonal produce for flavor and choose organic if possible (especially if you have any chronic health problems). Vary your fruit and vegetable choices and take advantage of the wide assortment available to us today.

Fruits– Both nutritious and economical. Many stores carry fresh fruit that has already been cleaned and cut for convenience. Don't rely solely on citrus and apples. Consider various melons, kiwi, mangoes, papaya, raspberries, etc. for variety. Unsweetened frozen fruits and those canned in their own juice are good staples to have on hand. Fruit juice is not a good choice for balance.

Vegetables– Choose fresh, frozen and canned (in that order). Visit the salad bar at your supermarket for convenience. Look for cauliflower and broccoli florettes, precut stir-fry vegetables and greens, especially organic, leafy greens, ready for tossing, in the produce section. A bag of mixed vegetables that have already been cleaned and chopped offer maximum convenience for tossing with fresh greens such as spinach anytime--even for breakfast! They can be served on the side or in an omelet. It's easy to find fresh, organic mixed greens at your local co-op or health food store. They're convenient and packed with healing nutrients.

The only canned vegetable you should use regularly is a canned tomato product. Again reading labels is important for a healing diet. Most canned tomato products (sauces, stewed, chopped or whole) are preserved with citric acid, grown commercially in a yeast base to which many people are sensitive. Look for tomato paste, spaghetti sauces, sun-dried tomatoes or tomato powder at your local health food store to add a robust tomato flavor to a meal without the citric acid. We have found a brand of chopped tomatoes from Italy, called Pomi, that come in a box with nothing added. The only ingredient is chopped tomatoes. They keep on the shelf until opened. Then they must be refrigerated and used within ten days.

Breads, Grains and Cereals

Bread– The best bread for blood sugar stabilization is 100% whole grain rye. You may have to search diligently to find rye bread without added wheat flour. There are two available in our area. In addition to being wheat free, they are also yeast free. One is made by French Meadow Bakery in Minneapolis; the other is imported from Canada.

If you are replacing two carbohydrate blocks (2 cups of vegetables or a piece of fruit) with a slice of bread, you'll want the most nutrient dense, whole grain bread you can find to give your body the most nutrition possible from that slice. Some of our favorites are made by Natural Ovens of Manitowoc, Wisconsin. High fiber, fresh, whole breads such as theirs, satisfy your hunger and don't trigger your carbohydrate cravings. Their breads contain no preservatives, no partially hydrogenated oil and no appetite stimulants. Trust us, it's mandatory to check the ingredient list when buying bread. Don't trust the marketing hype on the label. The first ingredient on most grocery store whole wheat or seven grain breads is enriched wheat flour.

A truly healthy muffin is a rare find. It's best to make these from scratch. Naturally, we have included a recipe for a healthy muffin that's high in protein. Whole wheat pita bread may save the day occasionally, especially for lunch, but most pitas list white, enriched flours the first ingredient and it takes only 1/2 a small one to make a block of carbohydrate.

Crackers– Wasa and Ryvita crackers are made from whole rye flour and are easy to find at major grocery chains. You may discover other whole grain flat bread type of crackers. Avoid highly processed crackers loaded with hydrogenated fat and sodium. It's totally amazing how many carbohydrates and fat grams are packed into just one small snack cracker!

Great Grains– Whole grains are the best. Many ethnic grains are available in the bulk food section at health food stores and prepackaged grains by such well known companies as Arrowhead Mills are usually found quite easily. We have listed these grains on both our shopping list and our block food list for that "adventurous cook" hidden within you. Check them out next time you are shopping in a health food store and take a chance on a new "old world" grain sometime soon.

Cereals– Again, whole grains make the best cereals for "staying power." Everyone is familiar with oatmeal. Whole oats or steel cut oats seem to hold best. Other whole grains to look for are: amaranth, barley, quinoa, kamut, spelt, teff, rye, buckwheat, wild rice, etc.

Bountiful Beans– Beans provide a powerhouse of high fiber carbohydrate and additional protein to your meal. When not using fresh or dried, look for canned, organic beans from the health food section of your grocery. They are the most nutritious choice. Sweet beans, the young green soybeans we talked about in the protein section, are now available in the freezer section of most major supermarkets. Companies such as Eden and Health Valley offer a wide variety of prepared, canned beans and chili. You may even be lucky enough to find fresh beans in the freezer section of your favorite grocery store. Sweet green soybeans, lima beans, butter beans, etc. are readily available.

Fats

As we've mentioned, there are two sources of fat in our diet. One source comes from animals, the other from plant oils. We will concentrate here on the fat we add to our food and the naturally occurring fats in seeds, nuts and dairy that are used to balance the protein and carbohydrate at a meal. Then we will briefly discuss the toxic fats that are sneaking into our processed foods.

Some of us are still eating more fat than we think, but many others are not eating enough, and its especially hard to get enough of the "good" fats we need to build those elusive eicosanoids. From a taste standpoint, fat carries the flavor of foods and spices to your taste buds and leaves you feeling satisfied at the end of a meal.

From a health standpoint, we now know, no-fat is not better than low fat. Unprocessed fats and oils are good for you when consumed in moderation. Thirty percent of your diet should come from fat. Remember, it's the quality, not the quantity, that is important. Your body needs essential fats for cell membrane formation, to provide fatty tissue to insulate and cushion your body, to boost your immune system, to absorb vitamins A, E, D, and K, to burn for energy, to produce eicosanoids (powerful hormones that affect your metabolism)

and to slow the release of sugar into your bloodstream.

There is another type of fat that does not occur naturally. This fat is altered through processing. We call this processed fat toxic fat because it has a toxic affect on our health and should be avoided. Refined, altered fats aggravate disease. Toxic fat includes margarine, vegetable shortening, partially hydrogenated vegetable oil, oils used in deep fat frying, and commercially processed, refined oils sold in clear glass containers on the shelves of your supermarket. These toxic fats contain trans fats which crowd out the natural, essential fats, damage our cells and interfere with our hormone functions. They also lack the vitamin E that's essential for keeping fats from oxidizing, becoming rancid, and damaging our blood vessels.

Highly processed, damaged fats are hidden in everything from lunch meats and salad dressings to innocent looking packaged rice dinners. Snack foods like chips and crackers and bakery goods such as cakes, pies and cookies, can also harbor hidden, processed unhealthy fat.

So for simple Zone planning, its best to avoid processed prepared foods and return to fresh, natural, whole foods. That way, your fat will come only from your lean protein choices and the oils, nuts and seeds you add intentionally to balance your meals and snacks.

The following tips will help you choose which ones to include in your diet. Our food list contains the health promoting fats we recommend to our clients.

Keep saturated fats to a minimum. These come from animal sources and from coconut, palm and palm kernel oils. However, these oils, along with butter, are better choices for high heat cooking than polyunsaturated oils which are damaged by heat. They are used safely in chocolate coatings on ice cream and candy, even on tofu ice cream bars at your health food store and in the coating on the 30/40/30 nutrition bars that are being marketed to help people stay in the Zone.

The fats you add to balance your meals should come mainly from the heart healthy monounsaturated fats in almond, walnut, canola, avocado, grape seed, macadamia nut and olive oils. A small-amount of these oils goes a long way in adding depth, bite or delicate flavor to various ethnic dishes, salad dressings or baked goods.

We recommend cold-pressed, unprocessed organic oils whenever possible. These are available in health food stores. Extra virgin olive oil is usually available in major grocery stores. Most grocery store oils contain additives, are highly processed and damaged, and cannot be used by your body in the important chemical reactions needed to maintain optimal health. These oils have been stripped of their beneficial substances, their energy--we call them dead fats! They also contain those toxic trans-fats that damage our cells and lead to the diseases of aging.

Preservative Free Ingredients

When using natural foods for optimum nutrition you also want to use preservative free sweeteners, sauces and marinades. Here are two interesting ingredients we use instead of artificial sweeteners and commercial soy sauce.

Vegetable glycerine–is derived from coconut oil by a process called hydrogenolysis, which takes off the fatty acids and leaves pure vegetable glycerine. It is non-toxic and easily digested. Though it is metabolized in the body like a carbohydrate, it does not cause an insulin response. Its warm, sweet taste makes it an excellent substitute for sugar. It adds sweetness to foods and baked goods without disrupting blood sugar levels.

Bragg Liquid Aminos– makes an excellent replacement for commercial soy sauce which may contain wheat, MSG or other additives people could be sensitive to. A natural blend of amino acids, the building blocks of protein, and soy, it can be substituted in any recipe calling for natural shoyu, tamari or miso. It adds great flavor to meats, salad dressings and stir fry.

Shopping List for Picture Book Recipes

Choose your favorite foods from this list to create your balanced building block meals.

PROTEIN
(30% of calories)

Meat and Poultry
(ORGANIC IS BEST)

beef, lean ground
(5-10% fat)
lean cuts:
   top round
   eye of round
   sirloin
   sirloin tip
chicken breast, skinless
duck
organic whole eggs
egg whites
ostrich
rabbit
turkey breast, skinless

Fish and Seafood
(FRESH, FROZEN OR WATER PACK, LOW SALT)

fish, any type
trout, canned in water
tuna, canned in water
salmon, canned
sardines
seafood:
   crab
   lobster
   scallops
   shrimp

Protein rich cheese
cottage cheese:
   Friendship 1%
   Old Home dry curd
   Breakstone's 2%
farmer's cheese, curds
mozzarella, part skim
ricotta, part skim

Vegetarian
Boca burgers

protein powder
soy burgers
soy flakes
soy hot dogs
soy milk, Westsoy organic
soy protein isolate
soy sausages
spirulina powder
tofu, firm and extra firm
   Mori-Nu
   White Wave organic
tofu powder
TVP
   (textured vegetable protein)

PROTEIN-CARBO-HYDRATE FOODS
buttermilk, low fat
milk, skim or 1%
sweet beans
   (frozen green soybeans)
soy milk:
   EdenSoy Original
tempeh
yogurt, plain, with active
   bacteria
yogurt, homemade
tofu soft and regular

CARBOHYDRATES
(40% of calories)
(FRESH, FROZEN, CANNED, UNSWEETENED IN OWN JUICE, ORGANIC IF POSSIBLE)

Fruits
apples
applesauce
apricots
blueberries
cherries
grapes
grapefruit
kiwi fruit
lemon
lime
melons
nectarines

oranges
peaches
pears
pineapple
plums
raspberries
strawberries
tangerines
watermelon

Lean, fibrous vegetables
(FRESH OR FROZEN, ORGANIC IF POSSIBLE)

artichoke
arugula
asparagus
bamboo shoots
bibb lettuce
beans, green or wax
bok choy
broccoli
brussels sprouts
cabbage
cauliflower
celery
chard
Chinese cabbage
cilantro
collard greens
cucumber
eggplant
endive
escarole
green onions (scallions)
hot peppers
jicama
kale
kohlrabi
leeks
potatoes, baking
potatoes, new red
potatoes:
   Mr. Dell's frozen
   hash browns
radicchio
radish
romaine lettuce
salsa

sauerkraut
shallots
snow peas
spinach
sprouts:
   alfalfa
   radish
   mung
squash:
   yellow
   crooknecked
   spaghetti
   zucchini
Swiss chard
tomatoes
tomatoes, sun dried
turnip greens
watercress

Canned tomato products:
(WITHOUT CITRIC ACID)

Pasta Sauce:
   Enrico's
   5 Brothers
   Classico
Pomi tomatoes

Beans and Legumes
(DRIED, FROZEN, CANNED ORGANIC)
black beans
black bean dip
chickpeas
   (garbanzo beans)
lentils
humus
sweet beans
   (frozen green soybeans)

Pasta, Cereals, Grains & Breads
barley, whole grain hulled
   (not pearl)
corn tortillas
kamut
oatmeal
steel cut oats
whole oats
quinoa

Ryvita crackers
spelt
Wasa crackers, lite rye
wild rice
whole grain rye bread
cracked or steel cut rye
whole rye berries
whole wheat pita bread

FAT (30% of calories)
(RAW NUTS, ORGANIC IF POSSIBLE & UNREFINED, COLD-PRESSED ORGANIC OILS)

almond butter
almonds, whole
almond oil
avocado
Brazil nuts
butter
canola oil
cream
flax seed oil

ghee
grape seed oil
guacamole
hazelnuts
macadamia nuts
macadamia nut oil
mayonnaise
    (cold-pressed canola oil)
Nayonaise
olive oil
olive oil and lemon juice dressings
olive oil and vinegar dressings
olives
pecans
pine nuts, raw
pumpkin seeds
sesame seeds
sunflower seeds
tahini
walnuts

walnut oil

MISCELLANEOUS & SUPPLEMENTAL PRODUCTS
Flavorings
Braggs liquid Aminos
garlic cloves
mustard– Dijon style
tomato paste (no citric acid)
tomato sauce (no citric acid)
tomato powder
raw, unfiltered vinegar
vanilla, pure extract

Sweeteners
fructose, crystalline
maple syrup
Memordica
molasses,
    medium unsulfured
vegetable glycerine

Protein Powders
Designer Protein–
    vanilla or chocolate
Genista soy protein
Protein Plus
Iso3 Protein Powder
Perfect Protein
Ultra Meal
Ultra Clear
Ultra Clear Sustain
Ultra Clear Plus

MISCELLANEOUS
Baking Needs
baking soda
baking powder, aluminum free
whole grain flours

Canned Broths
Organic chicken broth
Organic vegetable broth

Building Block Food List

PROTEIN BLOCKS
APPROXIMATELY 7 GRAMS OF PROTEIN PER BLOCK

Meat and Poultry
(organic preferred)

beef, ground
(10% or less fat), 1.5 oz.
Beef, lean cuts, 1.5 oz.:
    Top Round
    Eye of Round
    Sirloin
    Sirloin Tip
Buffalo,1 oz.
Chicken breast,
    skinless,1 oz.
Chicken, dark meat,
    skinless,1 oz.
Duck, 1.5 oz.
Egg, whites, 2
Egg, whole, 1
Lamb, lean, 1.5 oz.
Ostrich, 1 oz.
Rabbit, 1.5 oz.
Turkey breast,
    skinless, 1 oz.
Turkey, dark meat,
    skinless, 1.5 oz.

Veal, 1.5 oz.
Venison, 1 oz.

Fish and Seafood
Bass, 1.5 oz.
Bluefish, 1.5 oz.
Calamari,.1.5 oz.
Catfish, 1.5 oz.
Cod, 1.5 oz.
Clams, 1.5 oz.
Crab meat, 1.5 oz.
Haddock, 1.5 oz.
Halibut, 1.5 oz.
Lobster, 1.5 oz.
Mackerel, 1.5 oz.
Orange Ruffie, 1.5 oz.
Pike, Northern, 1.5 oz.
Salmon, 1.5 oz.
Sardines, 1 oz.
Scallops, 1.5 oz.
Shrimp, 1.5 oz.
Snapper, 1.5 oz.
Sole, 1.5 oz.
Swordfish, 1.5 oz.
Trout, 1.5 oz.
Tuna (steak), 1.5 oz.
Trout,
    canned in water, 1 oz.

Tuna,
    canned in water, 1 oz.

Dairy
Cottage cheese,
    dry curd, 1/4 cup
Cottage cheese,
    low fat, 1/4 cup
Cheese,
    reduced fat, 1 oz.
Farmers, 1/4 cup
Mozzarella, skim, 1 oz.
Ricotta,
    skim, 2 oz. or 1/4 cup
Parmesan, 2 tbsp.

Vegetarian
Protein powder, 1 tbsp.
Soy burgers, 1/2 patty
Soy hot dogs, 1 link
Unsweetened WestSoy
    100% organic
    soy milk, 8 oz.
Soy cheese, 2 oz.
Soy protein isolate, 1 tbsp.
Soy sausages, 2 links
Spirulina powder, 1 oz.
Tofu, firm, 3 oz.
Tofu spread, 6 tbsp.

TVP
(textured vegetable protein)
    Granules, 1/4 cup
    Flakes, 1/4 cup

PROTEIN-CARBOHYDRATE
(CONTAINS ONE BLOCK OF PROTEIN AND ONE BLOCK OF CARBOHYDRATE)

Original EdenSoy
    soy milk, 3/4 cup
Milk, skim or 1%, 1 cup
Sweet Beans, 3/4 cup
Tempeh, 1/4 cup
Yogurt, plain, 1/2 cup

CARBOHYDRATE BLOCKS
(APPROXIMATELY 9 GRAMS CARBOHYDRATE PER BLOCK)

Cooked Vegetables
Acorn squash, 1/4 cup
Artichoke, 1 small
Asparagus, 1 cup (12 spears)
Beans, green or wax, 1 cup
Beets, sliced, 1/2 cup
Bok choy, 3 cups
Broccoli, 1 cup

Brussels sprouts, 1 cup
Butternut squash, 1/3 cup
Cabbage, 1 1/2 cups
Carrots, sliced, 1/2 cup
Cauliflower, 1 1/2 cups
Chayote squash, 1 cup
Collard greens, 1 cup
Corn, 1/4 cup
Eggplant, 1 1/2 cups
Kale, 1 cup
Jicama, 1/2 cup
Leeks, 1 cup
Lima beans, 1/4 cup
Mushrooms, boiled, 1 cup
Okra, sliced, 1 cup
Onions, boiled, 1/2 cup
Parsnip, 1/3 cup
Peas, 1/3 cup
Potato, baked, 1/3 cup
Potato, boiled, 1/3 cup
Refried beans,
    vegetarian, 1/4 cup
Sauerkraut, 1 cup
Spinach, 1 cup
Sweet potato, baked, 1/3
Sweet potato, mashed, 1/5 cup
Swiss chard, 1 cup
Tomato, canned, 3/4 cup
Tomato paste, 1/4 cup
Tomato powder, 1/2 oz.
Tomato puree, 1/3 cup
Tomato sauce, 1/2 cup
Tomato, stewed, 1/2 cup
Tomato, sun dried, 1/4 cup
Turnip, mashed, 1 cup
Turnip greens, 1 1/2 cups
Yellow squash, 1 cup
Zucchini, 1 cup

Raw Vegetables

Alfalfa sprouts, 7 1/2 cups
Bean sprouts, 3 cups
Broccoli, 2 cups
Cabbage, shredded, 2 cups
Carrot, 1/3 cup
Cauliflower, 2 cups
Celery, sliced, 2 cups
Chayote, 1 cup
Cucumber, 1
Cucumber, sliced, 2 cups
Endive, chopped, 5 cups
Escarole, chopped, 5 cups
Green pepper,
    chopped, 1 1/2 cups
Green peppers, 2
Jicama, 1 cup
Lettuce, iceberg, 1 head

Lettuce, leaf, 4 cups
Lettuce, romaine,
    chopped, 4 cups
Mushrooms,
    chopped, 3 cups
Onions, chopped, 1 cup
Radishes, sliced, 2 cups
Salsa, 1/2 cup
Snow peas 1 cup
Spinach leaves, 4 cups
Spinach salad, 1 salad
    (2 cups spinach leaves, 1/4
cup raw onion, 1/4 cup sliced
radish , and 1/2 cup raw tomato)
Tomatillo, 6 oz.
Tomato, chopped, 1 cup
Tomatoes, 2
Tomatoes, cherry,
(8 medium), 1 cup
Tossed salad, 1 salad
    (2 cups organic greens, 1/4
cup raw green pepper, 1/4 cup
sliced zucchini, and 1/4 cup raw
tomato)
Water chestnuts, 1/3 cup

Fruits

Apple, 1/2
Applesauce, 1/4 cup
Apricots, 3
Banana, 1/3
Blackberries, 1/2 cup
Blueberries, 1/2 cup
Cantaloupe, 1/4 melon
Cantaloupe, cubed, 1 cup
Cherries, 7
Fruit cocktail, 1/2 cup
Grapefruit, 1/2
Grapes, 10 medium
Honeydew, cubed, 1/2 cup
Kiwi Fruit, 1
Lemon, 1
Lime, 1
Mango, sliced, 1/3 cup
Nectarine, 1/2
Orange, 1/2
Orange, mandarin,
    canned, 1/3 cup
Papaya, cubed, 1/2 cup
Peach, 1
Peaches, canned, 1/2 cup
Pear, 1/3
Pineapple, cubed, 1/2 cup
Plum, 1
Raspberries, 2/3 cup
Strawberries, 1 cup
Tangerine, 1
Watermelon, cubed, 1/2 cup

Beans and Legumes (cooked)

Adzuki, 1/2 cup
Anasazi, 1/2 cup
Black (turtle), 1/2 cup
Black bean dip, 1 tbsp.
Blackeye peas, 1/2 cup
Cannellini
    (white kidney), 1/2 cup
Chickpeas
    (garbanzos), 1/2 cup
Fava, 1/2 cup
Great Northern, 1/2 cup
Hominy, 1/2 cup
Hummus, 1/2 cup
Kidney, 1/2 cup
Lima, 1/2 cup
Mung, 1/2 cup
Navy, 1/2 cup
Pink, 1/2 cup
Pinto, 1/2 cup
Pinto bean dip, 4 tbsp.
Red, 1/2 cup
White, 1/2 cup
Yellow, 1/2 cup
Lentils, 1/4 cup
Peas, split, 1/4 cup

Grains & Bread

Amaranth, 1/4 cup
Whole Barley, 1/4 cup
Bread,
    Whole-Grain Rye, 1/2 slice
Buckwheat Groats, 1/4 cup
Kamut, 1/4 cup
Millet, 1/4 cup
Oat Groats, 1/2 cup
Steel-cut Oats, 1/2 cup
Rolled Oats, 1/2 cup
Pasta, cooked, 1/4 cup
Pita bread, mini, 1/2 pocket
Quinoa, 1/4 cup
Rice, brown, 1/4 cup
Rye Berries, 1/4 cup
Rolled Rye, 1/2 cup
Spelt, 1/4 cup
Teff, 1/2 cup
Tortilla,
    corn (6-inch), 1
Wild rice, 1/4 cup
Wheat:
    Bulgar, 1/4 cup
    Cracked Wheat, 1/4 cup
    Rolled Wheat, 1/4 cup
Crackers:
    Ryvita Light Crisp Bread,
    1-1 1/2 slices
    Ryvita Dark Crisp Bread,
    1-1 1/2 slices

Ryvita Original Snack bread,
    2 slices
Ryvita Sesame snack Bread,
    2 slices
Wasa Hearty Crisp Bread,
1 slice
Wasa Lite Rye Crisp Bread,
2 slices
Wasa Savory Crisp Bread,
2 slices
Wasa Whole Grain Crisp Bread,
2 slices

Other Carbohydrates

Fructose granules, 2 tsp.
Vegetable glycerine, unlimited

FAT BLOCKS
*(APPROXIMATELY 1.5 GRAMS
FAT PER BLOCK*

Almonds, raw whole, 3
Almonds, slivered, 1-1/2 tsp.
Almond butter,
    unroasted, 1/2 tsp.
Avocado, 1 tbsp.
Brazil nuts,
    raw whole, 2
Butter, 1/3 tsp.
Canola oil, 1/3 tsp.
Cream, half & half, 1 tbsp.
Cream, light coffee, 1/2 tbsp.
Cream, sour, 1/2 tbsp.
Cream cheese, 1 tsp.
Flax seed oil, 1/3 tsp.
Grape seed oil, 1/3 tsp.
Guacamole, 1/2 tbsp.
Hazelnuts, raw whole, 3
Macadamia nuts,
    raw whole, 1
Macadamia oil, 1/3 tsp.
Mayonnaise, light, 1 tsp.
Mayonnaise, regular, 1/3 tsp.
Nayonaise, 1/2 tbsp.
Olive oil, 1/3 tsp.
Olive oil and vinegar
    dressing, 1 tsp.
Olives, 3
Pecans, raw halves, 3
Pine nuts, raw. 1 tsp.
Pumpkin seeds, raw, 3/4 tsp.
Sunflower seeds, raw, 3/4 tsp.
Tahini, unroasted, 1 tbsp.
Walnuts, raw halves, 2

 **PROTEIN**
7 GRAMS

 **CARBOHYDRATE**
9 GRAMS

 **FAT**
1.5 GRAMS

BREAKFAST_____

2 ☐ ☐
3 ☐ ☐ ☐
4 ☐ ☐ ☐ ☐

SNACK_____

1 ☐
2 ☐ ☐

LUNCH_____

3 ☐ ☐ ☐
4 ☐ ☐ ☐ ☐
5 ☐ ☐ ☐ ☐ ☐

SNACK_____

1 ☐
2 ☐ ☐

DINNER_____

3 ☐ ☐ ☐
4 ☐ ☐ ☐ ☐
5 ☐ ☐ ☐ ☐ ☐

SNACK_____

1 ☐
2 ☐ ☐

BREAKFAST_____

2 ☐ ☐
3 ☐ ☐ ☐
4 ☐ ☐ ☐ ☐

SNACK_____

1 ☐
2 ☐ ☐

LUNCH_____

3 ☐ ☐ ☐
4 ☐ ☐ ☐ ☐
5 ☐ ☐ ☐ ☐ ☐

SNACK_____

1 ☐
2 ☐ ☐

DINNER_____

3 ☐ ☐ ☐
4 ☐ ☐ ☐ ☐
5 ☐ ☐ ☐ ☐ ☐

SNACK_____

1 ☐
2 ☐ ☐

BREAKFAST_____

2 ☐ ☐
3 ☐ ☐ ☐
4 ☐ ☐ ☐ ☐

SNACK_____

1 ☐
2 ☐ ☐

LUNCH_____

3 ☐ ☐ ☐
4 ☐ ☐ ☐ ☐
5 ☐ ☐ ☐ ☐ ☐

SNACK_____

1 ☐
2 ☐ ☐

DINNER_____

3 ☐ ☐ ☐
4 ☐ ☐ ☐ ☐
5 ☐ ☐ ☐ ☐ ☐

SNACK_____

1 ☐
2 ☐ ☐

BLOCK MEALS: Day_____

BREAKFAST:

Protein ☐ _____

Carbohydrate ☐ _____

Fat ☐ _____

SNACK:

Protein ☐ _____

Carbohydrate ☐ _____

Fat ☐ _____

LUNCH:

Protein ☐ _____

Carbohydrate ☐ _____

Fat ☐ _____

SNACK:

Protein ☐ _____

Carbohydrate ☐ _____

Fat ☐ _____

DINNER:

Protein ☐ _____

Carbohydrate ☐ _____

Fat ☐ _____

SNACK:

Protein ☐ _____

Carbohydrate ☐ _____

Fat ☐ _____

Recipe Index

Carolyn Brooks

Carolyn Brooks, B.S., co-founder of Nutritional Weight & Wellness and co-author of **Picture Book for Zone Cooks** *is a health educator, whole foods instructor, nutrition lecturer and writer. She is a Psychonutritional counselor with a focus on weight management, hormone balance, Candida and food allergies. Her passion is teaching people how to use food to promote healing. Assessing individual needs, she provides her clients with tools and motivation for change.*

Darlene Kvist

Darlene Kvist, M.S., C.N.S., L.N., is a Certified Nutrition Specialist, Licensed Nutritionist, co-founder of Nutritional Weight & Wellness and co-author of **Picture Book for Zone Cooks.** *She has 30 years of experience as an educator and psychonutritional counselor and enjoys the challenge of helping a broad range of clients with unique health needs and chronic conditions. Nutritional Weight & Wellness is a well-respected health education and nutritional counseling center in the Twin Cities area.*